From the
Peach Fields
to Becoming a
University Professor

How God strengthened me through my struggles
and turned my tears into a testimony

Dr. Barbara Searcy Cothran

ISBN 978-1-64140-734-2 (paperback)
ISBN 978-1-64140-735-9 (digital)

Christian Faith Publishing, Inc.
832 Park Avenue
Meadville, PA 16335
www.christianfaithpublishing.com

Printed in the United States of America

To my children, Dion Knox, and Kiara Loud.

I am so blessed that God gave me children such as you. Little did I know that one day the two of you would have to assure me that I was not weak, that I had raised and educated you primarily as a single parent while working two jobs in addition to going back to school to further my education.

Dion, thank you for the daily scriptures and the reminders that I was not being punished, but that God was preparing me for great things.

Of all of the mothers in the world, God gave the two of you to me, and now I know why. He knew what I would encounter and when. He gave me children that he knew would stand by me, support me, and still not have unforgiveness in their hearts toward others. I encourage the two of you to always be kind to others; even if they mistreat you, pray for then and be kind to them anyway. Remember that this is not a suggestion, it is a mandate from God. I love the two of you and thank you for loving me.

> *"Therefore I ask that you do not lose heart at my tribulations for you, which is your glory."*
> —*Ephesians 3:13*

"For I know the plans I have for you," says the Lord. "They are plans for good and not for disaster, to give you a future and a hope. In those days when you pray, I will listen. If you look for me wholeheartedly, you will find me."

—*Jeremiah 29:11–13*

CONTENTS

ACKNOWLEDGMENTS

I want to give all thanks to God who kept me, purged me, and gave me the inspiration to write this book. It was God who gave me this title, and I give all honor and praises to Him because I can say without a doubt that He is worthy.

There are so many others that I would like to thank for encouraging me to not necessarily write a book about my life, but who played an integral part in praying for and with me, reminding me that I am not who man say I am, but I am who God says that I am.

Dr. Clem Slack, I want to thank you for informing me of the position at Shorter and encouraging me to call the department chair to introduce myself even after the decision was made to hire the gentleman with the doctorate degree. I thank God that I was obedient because this call led to my invitation to give a teaching demonstration and being offered the job as assistant professor of education at Shorter College. I will never forget how we would stand in one of our offices and pray each day and many times during the day. But most importantly, your prayers and support during my depression and feelings of worthiness. Thank you.

I thank my children, Dion Knox and Kiara Loud, for standing by me and praying for me during some of the most difficult times in my life. You encouraged me to keep praying. Thank you, my daughter-in-law Demetria.

Pastor DeShannon Davis and Sister Judy Davis, I want to thank you for calling and praying with me and reminding me that I should take one baby step at a time. I love you along with the St. Paul Baptist Church family.

Pastor Carey Ingram, Bishop Howard World, Pastor Derrick Miler and Minister Star Miller, Minister Judy Curry, thank you for allowing God to use you in my healing.

An unnamed minister, thank you for your intercessory prayers and for constantly reminding me that God was giving me a ministry for working with women who are going through life-changing situations and to keep doing the right thing.

Thank you, Pastor Dale Levan and Wanda Lavan, for accepting me and supporting me.

Thank you to my biological sister, Loretta Searcy Terry, for taking care of me and allowing me to stay in your home when I felt I could not go on and was ashamed to return to my home.

To my sisters Ruth Jones and Virginia Jones, thank you for your prayers and support.

I want to personally thank in no particular order the following people that God sent to minister and support me and to be a reminder that He knows all and He sees all and that He would give me beauty for ashes.

Patsy Wade, I cannot thank you enough, my sister. You believed in me and you would not let me give up. You cried with me because you felt my pain.

To Denise Hill, I am certain that God sent you to our meeting on the exact day that I decided to return to our chapter meetings. For some reason, it was like we had known each other all our lives, and you took me under your wings and encouraged me to keep trusting God because He is in control.

Judy Ingram, I will always remember the numerous times that we talked and you continued assuring me that I was not the person that man said that I was. But when you said that you loved me and we would get through this together, I knew that God had sent you to me my sister. I will be eternally grateful to you.

To my best friend from elementary and high school, Ruth Harris, I want to thank you for your love and support. You encouraged me to keep trusting in God because He keeps his word and would heal me in His time.

And finally, there are others who I just want to thank for your support: Evelyn Hamilton, Wylodine Harrell, Drucella Henry, Carolyn Johnson, Costella Tiller, Barbara Ford, Brenda Sanford, Ernestine Payne, and others. You always used words to build me up and not tear me down. A friend is one who steps in when the whole world steps out. I love you all.

> *"Then they sat down on the ground with him for seven days and seven nights with no one speaking a word to him, for they saw that his pain was very great."*
>
> —*Job 2:13*

CHAPTER 1

My Birth

I knew you before I formed you in your mother's womb.

—*Jeremiah 1:5*

I was born one cold winter night in February to Willie (Big Baby) and Lizzie (Peaster) Searcy. How do I know this? My mom and dad told me about this as we sat around the dinner table on Sundays after coming home from church.

My mom and dad always joked about waiting years after they were married for a child, and then along I came with big beautiful eyes and a head full of curly hair. They also laughed about my dad rushing to get Ms. Mattie, who was the midwife in the small Southern town where I was born, to deliver me.

I remember being sick regularly from the time that I was about five years old. My mom was so afraid during these times that she could not bear to take care of me. She would send my dad down the street to bring Ms. Bertha to our house to take care of me and get my fever down. I was so frail, and I would often hear my parents talking about how I would always be a sickly child and I probably would not live to become an adult. My Mom would say that if I did live, I would never be able to work hard, so she began saving for me to go to college.

*"The Lord sustains him on his sick bed; in his illness
you restore him to full health" (Psalm 41:3).*

Many of the teachers boarded with families in my hometown
of Talbotton, Georgia, during the week. If they did not live a long
distance from Talbotton, they would go home each Friday afternoon
and return on Sunday night to begin their workweek of teaching.
I played school each day and at the age of five; one of the teachers
that boarded with my grandmother asked my mom if I could go to
school with her and be her helper. My mother gladly agreed. I was a
fast learner and I loved school. At the end of the school year, I had
learned everything that the first graders had been taught and much
more. I was promoted to the second grade along with the other students at the age of five. My parents never had to present the school
system with proof of my age, so I was the youngest student in my
class.

Second grade was as easy for me as first grade. I loved school,
and I wanted to go to school every day. I remember being sick a few
times during this school year, but for the most part, I missed very
little school. My favorite subjects were reading and English. I helped
other students in my class with reading, and this made me feel like a
little teacher.

Third grade was great, and I loved my teacher, Mrs. Lamar.
She was a heavyset lady who would hold us in her lap and love on
us all. Mrs. Lamar and her husband owned the only funeral home
in Talbotton, and she would often have all of us sit on the floor
around her and tell us stories about people sitting up in caskets and
the sounds that they made during the night. We were all amazed, and
oftentimes, I found it difficult to go to sleep at night. I have always
been afraid of the dark. These stories did not help me, but we all
enjoyed hearing them.

My favorite memories of third grade was stepping in the classroom and smelling collard greens cooking on top of the potbellied
heater. Mrs. Lamar would cook collard greens and meat to take home
for dinner while we were having class. It was so hard to concentrate
during these times because collard greens and cornbread was a favor-

ite food of mine. I was a picky eater, but oh, how I loved collard greens and cornbread. I still do to this day. Sometimes, Mrs. Lamar would take a spoon and let us taste the pot liquor from the collards. This was always delicious. Years after my third-grade year, I would smile and wonder how she had enough pot liquor in those collards to let us all taste some, using the same teaspoon.

Since Daddy worked on the railroad, he was away from home most of the time, but oftentimes he would get home from working late at night and go to the kitchen and cook up something called *goulash*. This consisted of leftovers that my mom kept in the refrigerator for such a time as when my daddy came home. We could smell this cooking all through the house, and my siblings and I would get up to eat this tasty dish.

Daddy loved to fish and hunt. I remember him catching brim, cleaning and cooking this fish, and making hush puppies and coleslaw to go with it. He would carefully pick the fish from the bones and give the meat to us to prevent us from swallowing bones. We all loved eating fish on Friday night. Daddy also cooked squirrel, rabbit, and occasionally coon meat. My siblings and I thought that we were eating fried chicken because this is what Daddy told us. Biscuits, grits, gravy, rabbit, squirrel (I mean fried chicken), and my mom's homemade preserves became a weekly meal for us, especially during the winter season.

All during my childhood, my parents would stress the importance of always telling the truth. Their favorite phrase was "If you lie, you will steal, and if you steal, you will kill." I never forgot this.

It was during my third-grade year that I learned division. I was so proud because math was not my strong subject, but my mom helped me at home so I was able to master not only division but multiplication as well. I was sick some during this academic year as I had been diagnosed with having convulsions (not an official diagnosis), but it appeared as though I was growing out of this. However, the motion sickness continued each time I rode in the back of the car for our weekly trip to Columbus. My dad always had to pull off the highway because I became nauseous.

Motion sickness was not fun at all. My siblings would stare at me as though to say, "You do this every time we get in the car." I could not help it. I became dizzy, nauseous, my head hurt, and many times I would have to regurgitate. This was not fun. Little did we realize that by sitting me in the front seat, the problem would have been resolved.

> *"Jesus looked at them and said, "With man it is impossible, but not with God. For all things are possible with God" (Mark 10:27).*

Fourth grade was fun also. I still loved school. Other than completing class work and homework, I mastered fractions. Remember, math was not my strong subject, but I always studied hard in order to stay ahead of my classmates. I often smile when I think about recess. Grades 1–12 had recess at the same time. When the bell rang, we all ran for the water fountain that consisted of a water pipe bent to form a spicket for drinking water.

One day, my cousin, a high school student, spent too much time drinking water. The line was long and the bell had already rung for us to be back in class. I don't know what motivated me to take my cousin's head and push it down on the faucet. When he turned around, I saw blood flowing from his mouth. He looked around at me, and I thought I was dead meat. He simply took his hand and covered his mouth. I later found out that when I pushed his head down, two of his teeth hit the faucet and broke off. I knew that I was in trouble at school and also with my parents. To my surprise, he did not report me to either the school or my parents. That was grace.

> *"For by grace you have been saved through faith. And this is not of your own doing; it is the gift of God" (Ephesians 2:8).*

CHAPTER 2

A Triple Tragedy

I have told you all this so you may have peace in me. Here on earth you will have many trials and sorrows. But take heart, because I have overcome the world.

—John 16:33

I was excited about starting fifth grade because I would be attending a newly built school for the black students in my hometown. I would no longer have to use outside toilets, and there were inside water fountains with clean, cold water. For the first time, I could go to the cafeteria and eat a hot lunch.

I lived approximately one mile from the new school. The board of education decided that they would not provide school buses for students who lived a mile or less from the school. I walked to school each morning and back home each afternoon. This was fun when it was warm. My father worked on the railroad and was not home several days during the week. My mother never learned how to drive, so during those extremely cold days and rainy days, my father paid a retired gentleman to drive my siblings and me to school. We were very blessed because all the other students that lived on "the hill" had to walk to and from school every day regardless of the weather.

Walking to and from school was fun, but at times this was extremely challenging. We were required to take all our textbooks home daily. Since we had no book bags, we were constantly dropping our books. Our teachers insisted that we wrap our books with brown paper even though they were already torn and battered.

One morning as I left home to walk to school, I felt something on my leg. When I looked down it was a snake that had crawled up my leg and had wrapped around it. I screamed and shook my leg so hard that it frightened the poor snake. I was told that it was a harmless chicken snake, but I feel that the only harmless snake is a dead snake. On cold days and rainy days, my father paid a retired gentleman to drive my siblings and me to school. We were very blessed because all the other students that lived on "the hill" walked to and from school every day.

At this time I had one brother and two sisters. Willene was born in January of my fifth-grade year. She was named after my father because she looked so much like him. I had so much fun holding her and playing with her.

One day, my mom and dad took my sister Loretta to the doctor because she had a bad cold. Since Willene appeared to be coming down with a cold, they asked the doctor to give her a checkup to make sure she was okay. The doctor put Willene in the hospital, and the next day, she passed away. This devastated all of us because she was not sick. We later found that she had an enlarged heart. We had no pictures of her, so the mortician took pictures of her in her casket. This was the first tragedy for me as a child, and what a tragedy it was.

> *"But Jesus said, 'Let the little children come to me and do not hinder them, for to such belongs to the kingdom of heaven'" (Matthew 13:14).*

I began my sixth-grade year with a sorrowful heart, but my sixth-grade teacher, Ms. Johnson, who later became Mrs. Yancy, took me under her wing and began to mentor me. I continued to love school, but I did not study as hard as I had previously. I remember how Mrs. Yancy would tell us how she had eyes in the back of her head and could see everything we were doing. For some reason, we believed this because she would have her back turned to the class, writing on the chalkboard, but she could call students by their names and ask them to stop playing without even looking around. That was weird.

It was during my sixth-grade year that my father bought me a baby grand piano and told me that I would be taking piano lessons. I enjoyed the days that I took piano lessons after school. I can remember practicing at least one hour each day, and I became pretty good at playing simple songs. I wanted to play rock and roll, but my father insisted that I only play by music. On the days when my parents went down the street to visit my grandparents, I learned how to play a song by Gladys Knight. To my knowledge, my father never found out that I could play a few songs "by air."

I will always remember my seventh-grade year. It was during this year that students from Woodland and Geneva were bused to the school in Talbotton. I met my lifetime friend, Ruth Harris.

*"A friend is always a friend, and relatives are born
to share our troubles" (Proverbs 17:17).*

My seventh-grade teacher was very strict. She made us walk the chalk line, and she gave us loads of homework. Once when she assigned the Gettysburg Address for us to learn, I decided that this was too much for me, so I did not learn it. When she called me to stand and recite the Gettysburg Address, of course I did not know it. I was given numerous lashes on my back with a strap. Needless to say, I was given a few additional days to learn the Gettysburg Address; and to this day, I can still recite it. That was a learning experience for me.

*"Let the wise hear and increase in learning, and the
one who understands obtains guidance" (Proverbs 1:5).*

My mother was the best cook. I remember how she would make chocolate fudge with nuts, divinity and tea cakes and wrap each one neatly in wrapping paper and send me around the community to sell these goodies for the church. She loved working for her church, St. Phillip AME. She would also make pound cake, and I would take slices around the community to sell in order to raise money for the church. My favorite desert, other than tea cakes, was her lemon cheesecake and caramel cake. I have not found anyone yet that could come close to making cakes like my mother did.

In November of my seventh grade, tragedy struck again. My grandfather, who had been ill for a while, passed away. My mother was close to him. Even though he was not her biological father, he and my grandmother had raised her after the death of her mother.

As a custom, when someone died, people in the community would go to the home of the deceased and sit with the surviving family members. My mom and dad walked across the street to my grandparents' home to sit with all the family members. I remember my mother coming home and getting in bed. She called down to my grandmother's and asked to speak to my dad and told him she did not feel well and that he needed to come home. My dad did not realize that she was that ill, so he stayed down to my grandmother's with the other members of the family and friends. After a period, my mother told me to go down to my grandmother's and tell my dad that he needed to come home immediately because she was sick. I remember running down the hill in the dark and to tell Daddy that Mama needed him to come and take her to the doctor. This got his attention, and he quickly got up, and we rushed back home. When we got there, it was obvious that my mom was quite ill, so my dad got her in the car to take her to Manchester to the doctor. We did not have a doctor in Talbotton, and Manchester is approximately fifteen to twenty miles from Talbotton.

Since I was the oldest, I was told to look after my younger siblings. I was only eleven, so I was a child myself. After about five minutes, I heard a car pull back in the yard; and to my surprise, it was Daddy bringing Mama back. He told me he got down the road, and Mama said, "Oh Lord, please don't let me leave my children," and she then passed out.

Many doctors in Manchester made house calls, so Daddy got Mama out of the car and back in bed. He then called for the doctor to come to our house. This took quite a while, but eventually, the doctor arrived. I could not hear what the doctor was saying, but after he left, I went and sat by Mama's bed. I remember talking to her for a while, and then she told me to go to bed. I heard her ask Daddy what the doctor said was wrong with her, but I did not hear Daddy's response. Daddy came in our room and told me to put on some clothes because he was taking me down to stay with Mrs. Pugh for the night. I had no idea why he had me to leave. The next morning, when I got back home, Mama was not there. I later found out that after Daddy took me down to the Pugh's, he then took Mama to St. Francis Hospital in Columbus, Georgia.

Daddy came home to get a change of clothes because he was going to stay with Mama, but before he could get back to Columbus, he received a call informing him that Mama had passed. That was one of the worst days of my life. We later found out that she had had a brain aneurysm. I did not know what that was; all I knew what that my mom was no longer with us. So, my grandfather died on a Saturday night, and my mother died that following Monday. Lord, have mercy.

"Blessed are those who mourn, for they will be comforted" (Matthew 5:4).

As my father prepared for my mother's homegoing services, the family was concerned about what would happen to all of us. My father worked on the railroad and was away from home at least five days out of the week. I was eleven, my sister Jacqueline was eight, Greg was six, Loretta was four, and Margaret was two months old. What would happen to us?

"So do not fear, for I am with you; do not be dismayed, for I am your God. I will strengthen you and help you; I will uphold you with my righteous right hand" (Isaiah 41:10).

Daddy had eight sisters and brothers, so it was decided that each one of them would choose one of us to raise, but Daddy was adamant about keeping us all together. He decided to hire a relative to stay with us when he was working. This worked for a while.

I remember Daddy sitting with me at the kitchen table and showing me how to write out money orders and checks to pay the bills. He took me to the bank and put my name on accounts. I had to learn adult responsibilities at the age of eleven—all except cooking. That never interested me.

In February, a little before my twelfth birthday, my siblings and I were sitting on the sofa watching television when my father walked in and introduced us to our new mother. We were shocked, and so were my mother's family. Thus began a new journey in all of our lives. My stepmother had three daughters of her own from a previous marriage, but we learned that they would remain with her mother and father that lived about one mile from where we lived. In October of that year, we welcomed a new baby brother, James, to the family.

It was difficult being the oldest of my siblings. Anytime my parents were not home, I was left in charge of my younger siblings. Although I tried to keep them under control, they would not mind me because they were almost the same age as I was. Regardless, if anything was broken or if any of my siblings were injured, guess who was blamed? *Me!*

CHAPTER 3

My First Job – Picking Peaches

As I approached the end of my seventh grade, I found myself missing my mom very much. I missed the way that she always ironed my dresses for school and combed my hair each day. I missed her cooking, and I missed seeing her as she cleaned the house each week. I remember seeing my mom get down on her knees to scrub our floors.

My grades began to slip as I could not concentrate on my studies. I always heard my mom tell my dad that I would never be able to work at any job that was hard, so she wanted me to get a college education. She actually began saving money for my education. Although my mom only worked for Mrs. Slade, cooking, cleaning, and seeing after her children, she managed to save a little each week for my education.

It was the summer between my seventh and eighth grade in school that I decided to get a job. In the small town of Talbotton, there was nothing for an African American girl or boy to do except pick cotton or pick peaches. During peach season, I asked my dad if I could get a job picking peaches. He quickly told me that I would not be able to manage staying out in the hot sun all day. I begged and begged until he gave in and said yes. I woke up early the next morning, fixed my lunch, and headed up the hill to catch the peach truck. Little did I realize what I was in for.

Both children and adults rode on the back of the large truck to Mr. Frank's peach orchard. Mr. Frank explained to us that there would be no playing around and that we would work from 6:00 a.m. To approximately 5:30–6:00 p.m. We would be paid $2.50 per day providing our peaches were not green, overly ripe, or bruised. (One of his sons would inspect our peaches as we poured the peaches from or buckets into crates.) We would have one hour for lunch.

Mr. Frank continued to explain to us that we were not to sit and rest under the peach trees or we would be fired. We were told that we would continue working even if it started to rain. We would be picked up and taken to his tenant's house only if there was a storm with thunder and lightning. That was frightening to me because I had always been afraid of storms. My mother's biological mother had been killed by lightning, so whenever there was a storm, my mother would take us to MaMa's house. If we were caught at home during the storm, my mother would unplug all the utilities; and depending on how serious the storm was, she would take us all in the bathroom, and sometimes we would all get under the bed.

I remember my first day picking peaches. After the sun came up, I thought I would pass out from the heat. My face, neck, and arms began to burn from the fur on the peaches. I was not told to wear long sleeves. There was no water in the fields. Approximately once each hour, the "water boy" would come around with a bucket of water that contained no ice and only one dipper for all of us to drink from. I remember seeing the ladies who dipped snuff drink from the dipper with the snuff in their mouths, but for some reason, I never thought much about it. When the "water boy" got to me, I was so thirsty, I gladly drank water from the dipper.

> *"There will be a shelter to give shade from the heat by day, and refuge and protection from the storm and the rain" (Isaiah 4:6).*

There were no bathrooms in the peach fields, so we had to wait until Mr. Frank picked us up for lunch and take us to one of his tenants' house in order for us to use the outside toilet. Many times, we had to eat our lunches in the peach field sitting under a peach tree. Our Double-Colas were hot, but they were delicious because we had something wet in our mouths.

I quickly learned how to tell when it was approaching lunch-time by standing in the sun. If I could see my shadow and put my foot directly on my head, I knew it was approaching lunchtime.

I remember eating peaches all during the day that were big and ripe. My favorite were Alberta peaches. They were always very juicy and sweet. I picked peaches, and I ate peaches, but I never got sick from eating peaches. I even sneaked peaches home, peeled them, sprinkled sugar over them, poured milk over them and enjoyed peaches and milk. I believe this is why I have no taste for fresh peaches today.

Around five thirty or six o'clock, I heard the truck driving up to pick all of us up to take us back to the corner where we would walk home. Mr. Frank called the roll to make sure we had worked a full day. I had passed the test. I had managed to work in the hot sun all day without getting sick. Now it was time to take a bath, eat, and go to bed. My first day working proved to be successful, but oh, was I tired, and it seemed as though my entire body was burning from the peach fur and from being in the hot sun almost twelve hours.

I picked peaches each summer to make money to help purchase my school clothes. I even picked okra after the peach season ended; however, I decided that picking peaches and okra would not be my lifelong profession. My dream was to become a medical doctor; or so I thought.

"For I know the plans I have for you, declares the Lord, plans for welfare and not for evil, to give you a future and a hope" (Jeremiah 29:1).

CHAPTER 4

Crow

Let no unwholesome word proceed from your mouth, but only such a word as is good for edification according to the need of the moment, so that it will give grace to those who hear.

—*Ephesians 4:29*

I was excited about going to eighth grade because I was considered a high school student. High school was so different. We changed classes, and the work was a lot harder. We were left unsupervised most of the time, and this gave "bullies" an opportunity to humiliate those of us who were shy.

I was extremely shy, and I remember crying each day as I walked home from school because there were bullies that called me "crow." The bullies were high school boys who were trying to impress some of the high school girls at my expense. I was called crow because of my skin color. It was during this time that I began to hate the color of my skin. I did not like being bullied every day. These high school boys would shout "Crow," flap their arms like the wings of a crow, and make sounds like a crow. I cried many nights at the thought of going to school the next day because I knew what to expect on my way home. Would my struggles ever end?

*"So whatever you wish that others would do to you,
do also to them, for this is the law and the prophets"
(Matthew 7:12).*

I found that there was a cream that would lighten my skin, so I went to the drugstore to purchase it. After reading the directions, I knew that this was what I needed to be accepted and not be called crow" anymore.

I rubbed this cream on my face every night. There was a slight burning, but I ignored the burning because this cream was going to change my life, and that it did. After about a week and a half, I noticed light spots appearing all over my face, but I continued to use the cream. One morning, I got up and went in the bathroom to get washed up for school. When I looked in the mirror, my face looked like a leopard. What should I do now? I knew that I would be the laughingstock of the school, but I had no choice but to go to school.

Of course, I was laughed at, and the bullies not only called me crow, but they called me spot as well. I decided that I would rather be one color than to have a spotted face, so I threw the remainder of the cream in the trash. After about two weeks, my face was back to its original color. Never again would I try and change the skin color that God gave me.

*"Do not judge by appearance, but judge with right
judgment" (John 7:24).*

I eventually learned to ignore the bullies. Although I tried to pretend that I was not upset by what those bullies called me, trust me, it hurt me deeply. I never tried to get them in trouble, and neither did the other students that walked home and heard and saw how they bullied me. I now understand that the other students were grateful that it was me and not them. My struggles continued.

There was an incident that happened during my eighth-grade year. I did not feel that is was funny during the time that this incident happened. All the girls wore half-slips and I wanted a half-slip also. My dad always took my siblings and me shopping for clothes, and he told me that I was too skinny to hold a half-slip up, so he would not buy me one. This made me sad because all the girls in my class and my cousins had half-slips.

I decided to cut my all-over slip off and make my own half-slip. I was so proud to finally be just like the other girls in my class. (We all showed off our hip slips in the girls' restroom.) Since I made my own hip slip, I used safety pins to pin my slip up. This worked for a while.

It was on the day that I wore my hip slip to school that we were doing a mock play during literature class. I was called up to the front to read one of the parts. After I had been standing for a while, I felt my slip slowly coming down. Surely it was not going to fall on the floor. As I continued to read my part, the inevitable happened. My slip fell to the floor in front of the entire eighth grade class. How embarrassing!

After I discovered what had happened, and with the class falling over with laughter, I stepped out of my slip, picked it up from the floor, and asked my teacher if I could go to the restroom and put my slip back on. She said that I could, so I walked to the restroom carrying my slip in my right hand.

After making sure that I had my slip pinned on me properly, I walked back in class totally embarrassed. There was a lesson to be learned here: always use elastic when making a hip slip because safety pins do not always keep things from safely falling off you.

"Hear, my son your father's instructions, and forsake not your mother's teachings" (Proverbs 1:8).

I never received a new textbook the entire time that I was in school. The "colored" school was given the old books passed down from the "white" school. The majority of the pages were torn and scribbled on. There were so many inappropriate drawings and racist remarks in our textbooks until many times, the information to be studied was illegible.

I played basketball all during my high school years. Our school had no gym, so we practiced outside on the ground. If it was extremely cold or raining, we practiced in the lunchroom. Of course, we never knew how it felt to practice on a gym floor, so when we played other schools, we would slip, slide, and most times we would fall because we could never get a feel for the gym floor. This brought about laughter from the spectators, but our coaches stood tall and straight and encouraged us to play hard. To my knowledge, we never won a game.

My cousin Estella was several grades ahead of me in school, but she always tried to look after me and tell me things that her mother had shared with her about the Searcy family. We would often talk about my mother's cooking and how she would always get down on hands and knees when she cleaned floors. I enjoyed those conversations with my cousin.

Daddy had a rule that if we did not attend Sunday school and church, we could not go to the cafe. This was a hangout for all the teenagers and adults, and it was within walking distance from our house. All the teenagers that lived on the "hill" would get together on Sunday afternoon and walk to Mr. Len's cafe. We were only allowed to go to the cafe on Sundays because Saturday and Saturday nights were basically reserved for adults. We knew that we were to be home before dark, and when we lost track of the time, Daddy would drive to the cafe to get us. This was so embarrassing, but all the girls from the hill would get in Daddy's car, and he would drop each one off at their homes.

Being the oldest of my siblings was difficult. Daddy was extremely strict on me. He reluctantly allowed me to have a boyfriend, but he could only come to see me on Sundays and at 9:00 p.m., if he had not left, Daddy would stick his head in the door and say, "It's time to go." This was embarrassing; however, my siblings were in the room because they were looking at our only television set. Daddy even threatened to accompany me to the prom.

When I turned sixteen, I got my driver's license. Although we only had one car, I was able to use it often when Daddy was working because my stepmother could not drive. I drove to Columbus to get McDonald's hamburgers and fries, to Columbus Mall, and all around Talbotton with my cousins and my sister Jack in the car with me. They never realized what danger they were in. I never realized how God was protecting us all.

There was a place called the Blue Hole, located outside of Talbotton, and we discovered it one day when my cousins, siblings, friends, and I decided that we would pack a lunch and find a picnic spot. This spot was clean with shade trees and a swimming hole. Everybody enjoyed getting in the water, but I could not swim so I watched while they played in the blue water. There was also a spot that had soft sand, and one day, one of my cousins stepped in this sand, and she began to sink deeper and deeper in the sand. With quick thinking, all of us got a stick and carefully handed it to her, and we were able to get her pulled out of the sinkhole. We had no idea how dangerous this was and how we could have lost our lives because we were out in the woods with no way of getting help quickly. Although we continued to go to the "Blue Hole," we avoided the sinkhole. Again, God protected us because no one ever drowned and none of us were swallowed up in the sinkhole.

"God is our refuge and strength, an ever-present help in trouble" (Psalm 46:1).

The remainder of my high school years were spent going to Sunday school and church on Sundays, going to school, taking piano lessons, going to basketball practice, and trying to decide what college I wanted to attend after graduating from high school. It was always an expectation that my siblings and I would go to college. My mother had saved money for me to attend college so I would not have to apply for student loans.

My father was the first African American policeman and city councilman in the small city of Talbotton. We were very proud of his accomplishments as he often told us that he only had a seventh-grade education because he had to quit school to help his father take care of the family. He was also a deacon and treasurer at Shady Grove

Baptist Church. He later became chairman of the deacon board and remained chairman until his health declined.

My father talked to us about the various jobs that he had worked on and how he persevered and was able to get a job as an engineer on the railroad. This job paid enough for my father to provide for six children. We did not have everything that we wanted, but we had the things that we needed.

I remember my father studying every spare moment for a mandatory test that all railroad engineers had to take in order to keep their jobs. My father had been employed as an engineer for over twenty-five years. This was his life. I would sit down at the kitchen table and quiz him on the questions that might be on the test. He was very nervous the day of the test because the majority of the other men were younger with a high school education and beyond. God was with my father because he passed this test with flying colors. What a mighty God we serve!

My father talked to me so much about life. He talked to me about managing money, that I should have a savings account for a "rainy day," that I should always pay my bills on time, and that a person's word should be their bond. At that time, I did not understand any of these, but upon becoming an adult, I learned to appreciate all of my father's advice. Little did I realize that I would give my children and the students that I taught the same advice.

*"Train up a child in the way he should go.
Even when he is old, he will not depart from it"
(Proverbs 22:6).*

My father had built our house that contained two bedrooms, a kitchen, living room, and bath before I was born. We were the only African American family with an inside bathroom for many years. We were also fortunate to have a television set. I can remember all the neighbors coming to our house to look at the television. Although we welcomed the company, it was tiring at times because we could not go to bed until they had all left.

During this time, my siblings and I slept in the same bedroom. There was a full-sized bed in the room, a twin-sized bed, and my brother slept on a roll-away bed. My baby brother James slept in a baby bed in the room with my parents, so my father built two more rooms in our house with closets in each room. We were very thankful to finally have more space and some privacy.

"By wisdom a house is built. And by understanding it is established" (Proverbs 24:3).

CHAPTER 5

A Difficult Decision

But the plans of the Lord stand firm forever, the
purpose of his heart through all generations.
—Psalm 33:11

Graduation was approaching, and I had to decide where I would attend college. I knew that I did not want to attend the college that was close to home and where the majority of students from Talbotton attended, but I needed to make a decision.

At the last minute, I applied to Savannah State and was accepted. My high school was not accredited, so I was required to take a series of exams to determine if I would be placed in remedial courses where I would not earn any credit. This was frightening to me because I had been a fairly good student in high school.

In August, my parents drove me to Savannah State for orientation. I was assigned a room in the dormitory on the third floor, and my two roommates were childhood friends from Dublin, Georgia. Since they were the first to be assigned to the room, they chose the two bottom bunks, so I was forced to sleep on the top bunk. This did not go over well with me, but I vowed that I would make the best of it.

During orientation, I learned about the campus, what majors were offered, where the cafeteria was located, and other important information about the school. There was a session where we were told about fees and when they were due. I was assigned an advisor, after which, I was taken to a room to begin taking a series of entrance exams. I remember being given a hat, and I was told to wear this each day during orientation. All freshmen were referred to as crabs. I did not know anyone at Savannah State, and I cried and begged my daddy to come and get me. He would just tell me to stay down there because it would get better.

The day for freshmen to register finally arrived. We stood in a long line to pay our fees, after which, we stood in another long line to talk to our advisor and get our classes. This process was long and tedious, but this was prior to the process that is in place today. I was a little nervous as I listened to students talk about their high schools and the scholarships that they were awarded.

As I talked to my advisor, she explained my schedule of classes and where they were located on campus. To my surprise, I had passed all my exams and would not need to take any remedial classes. I smiled from ear to ear. This small-town girl that graduated from an unaccredited high school with no gym was just as bright as the students that I heard bragging about their scholarships while standing in line to register. God was still looking out for me.

Being away from home and on my own for the first time was a challenge for me. I learned how to play bid whist. That was so much fun. I would stay up until all hours of the morning playing cards. I was grown now and could go to bed when I wanted to. Each Sunday, a cigarette salesperson would come to the girls' dormitory and give out packs of sample cigarettes. Some of the girls had smoked for years, but I had no desire to smoke. After thinking about this for a while, I decided that I wanted to go back home as a smoker so that all my family and friends would know that I was "grown." That was a big mistake. I tried smoking and inhaling a cigarette. My head began to hurt, I coughed, I became nauseated, and I was sick to my stomach for the remainder of the day. That was my first and last attempt trying to smoke. I decided to stick to eating chocolate cake.

On weekends, many of the students would go home. Since I lived too far away to go home often, I was invited to go home with my roommates to Dublin, Georgia. It was so good to eat home-cooked food and to get away from the noise in the dormitory.

There was one pay phone on each floor of the dormitory, so we were to limit our calls to three minutes. Daddy told me that I could call home once a week, so I took advantage of this because I was still homesick. I did not have the money or the clothes that the other girls had. Daddy had to provide for my siblings and take care of the bills. He would send me a little money every two weeks so that I could purchase toiletries and other personal items. I was still blessed because my friends would always include me when they went out to eat or when they purchased food. We would swap clothes—or rather, my friends would allow me to borrow their clothes.

All students living in the dormitory at Savannah State were required to attend vesper services each Sunday afternoon. Vesper was a church service that was geared to no particular faith. One hour of credit was given for successfully attending vesper services. Some students skipped vesper, and to their surprise, a grade of F was given. Since I did not have anyone telling me to get up and get ready for Sunday school and church, I slept in on Sundays, went to the dining hall for lunch, and lounged around until it was time to get ready for vesper.

My first semester away from home was coming to a close. There were final exams to study for. I had been neglecting my studies while spending too much time playing cards. I thought that I could pass my exams easily; however when I saw the number of questions, problems, true/false on my finals, I knew that I was in big trouble. Needless to say, my grades were not good that semester.

I don't know when my plans changed from wanting to be a doctor, but I imagine it was during my first semester when I took Biology 101. My professor explained to the class that our lab assignment was to dissect a rat. When we were shown the rats, I almost passed out. These rats were as large as cats. I could not stand the smell of the formaldehyde that kept the rats preserved. Although I used gloves, that smell remained on my hands for days; and to make matters worse, I went from biology to the dining hall for lunch. How could I possibly be a doctor when I could not even dissect a rat? My partner was a biology major, and I did as little as possible in the lab, touching the rat only when he asked me to hold it down so that he could dissect it. I passed that class with a D, so I knew that I would change my major when I returned to school after Christmas.

I was happy to see my family and friends when I arrived home for my Christmas break. Daddy gave my siblings and me some money to purchase a few items for ourselves. We shopped in Columbus because there were no department stores in Talbotton. I knew that I wanted a black suit. All the girls at Savannah State had black suits, and I wanted one also. I remember going to the Diana Shop and purchasing my black suit. I then went to Baker's and purchased a pair of black spool heels. I couldn't wait to go back to school so that I could wear my new black suit.

> *"It is the Lord who goes before you. He will be with you; he will not leave you or forsake you. Do not fear or be dismayed" (Deuteronomy 31:8).*

CHAPTER 6

Graduation at Last

Keep hold of instruction; do not let go; guard her, for she is your life.

—Proverbs 4:13

I went back to Savannah State year after year with no desire to graduate. After changing my major three times, I finally decided that I wanted to major in sociology. My goal now was to become a social worker, but first, I had to graduate.

I remember Daddy sitting me down for a heart-to-heart talk about school. He told me that I needed to either get serious about my studies and stop wasting his money or drop out and get a job. What an eye-opener that was. I had a flashback of the times when I picked peaches in the scorching sun and later working in the peach-packing shed. That flashback was enough for me to get serious about my studies, stop playing cards until all hours of the morning, and map out my plans for completing my education.

I began registering for a full load instead of the twelve hours that I had been accustomed to taking. This was hard work because I had already taken all of the easy classes. Now I knew what it meant to burn the "midnight oil."

I worked extremely hard because I was determined to make up for the time that I had wasted playing cards and neglecting my studies. After getting serious about my studies, I began to go to the library, study and prepare for my assignments and exams, and I made the dean's list or honor roll each semester. I knew that I needed a break, but I needed to make a decision whether to attend summer school to complete my requirements for graduation or wait until the fall semester and graduate in December. I decided to attend summer school and hopefully graduate in August.

Finally, the day came when I was approved for graduation. What a day that was. I knew that it was God who had brought me through, and all I could do was thank Him. I also know that Daddy and my family were all proud of me as I had finally fulfilled the dream that my mother had for me.

I graduated in August, after completing summer school. After the ceremony, we gathered all my belongings from the dormitory and headed back to Talbotton. I had obtained a degree, but I had no job. I had no idea what I was going to do. In order to get a job as a social worker, I would have to relocate to a larger city. We never know how God is going to work in our lives.

"But as for you, be strong and do not give up, for your work will be rewarded" (2 Chronicles 15:7).

CHAPTER 7

A Teaching Career and Marriage

Exactly one day after I arrived home from graduating from Savannah State, I received a phone call from my friend and former roommate, JoAnn Pritchett. It was so good hearing from her. She asked if I had a job, and I told her I did not. She said that there was an opening at Kingston Elementary School teaching and that I should call Mrs. Wheeler, later known as Dr. Wheeler, and apply for the job. I had no idea how to teach. I had no desire to teach, but God had other plans.

"Many are the plans in the minds of man, but it is the purpose of the Lord that will stand" (Proverbs 19:21).

Reluctantly, I called Mrs. Wheeler, and she hired me sight unseen. I didn't know what to think. She told me to report to Kingston School that Monday morning to begin teaching. This was Saturday, so I told Daddy about the job, but he wasn't happy about me going to work in a place where I did not know where I would be living. I told him that I knew Joanne and she had said that I could stay with her family.

On Sunday, I boarded the Trailways bus and headed to Cartersville where Joanne would pick me up and take me to her home in Kingston. I had visited Kingston at least once or twice prior to this time because I spent the weekend with Joanne when we were college roommates. I was not a stranger to the family, and they all welcomed me and made me feel a part of their family.

On Monday morning, I reported to Kingston School for my class assignment. I was assigned a first- and second-grade combination class. I had no idea how to teach students writing, reading, or anything else, but I used the *Teacher's Editions*, and I gladly accepted the help and advice from the veteran teachers.

I met Sandra Solomon, then Sandra Lavette, who taught the upper grades. The fifth, sixth, seventh, and eighth graders changed classes, and Ms. Lavette taught English. She was an excellent English teacher, and all the students loved her. She was the first African American teacher at Kingston School, and I was the second.

In addition to learning how to teach, I was introduced to pinto beans. I was raised on butter beans, so I had never seen or tasted pinto beans before. I remember JoAnn cooking pinto beans, cornbread, slaw, and fried chicken. I hesitated on eating the pinto beans because I did not know what they were or how they tasted, but after tasting them, I simply fell in love with them.

I made it through my first year of teaching, but I knew that teaching in the lower grades was not a good fit for me. I talked to my principal and asked if I could be moved to the upper grades the following year. At that time, there were no openings, but God was looking out for me. The teacher that taught social studies decided that she would retire, and I was moved to sixth grade the following year. Ms. Lavette transferred to Cass High School because she wanted to work with high school students.

I went back to Savannah State that first summer to take education classes in order to apply for my teaching certificate. I took four classes (twenty hours) and made all As. When I showed my grades to my dad, he asked why I couldn't make those grades when he was paying for my schooling. I smiled and did not answer, but I was thinking, *Now we are playing with my money. I couldn't waste my hard-earned money.*

I was able to purchase my first car during the summer. This gave me an opportunity to teach and take classes in the afternoon to complete the final education classes in pursuit of my teaching certificate. I enrolled at Berry College and Shorter College. By the end of the semester, I was able to apply for my professional T-4 certificate. What a blessed day it was when I was able to request transcripts from Savannah State, Berry, and Shorter to be sent to the State Board of Education as verification of my completion of the required education classes.

It did not take long for my professional T4 certificate to get back. I quickly drove to the superintendent's office in Cartersville and proudly presented them with my certificate. This would enable me to receive more money as I no longer had a probationary certificate. When I received my check for February, to my surprise, the county made my pay retroactive from the beginning of that school year. What a blessing!

"But my God shall supply all your need according to his riches in Glory by Christ Jesus" (Philippians 4:19).

I learned so much about teaching and specifically about the historic city of Kingston from Mrs. Margie Hood, who served as the school librarian. Mrs. Hood taught me how to keep my class register, and she brought me books with activities to use to enhance my teaching.

I was teaching social studies to grades 4–8, and this was ironic because I disliked social studies when I was in school, but now I loved it and loved teaching it to my students. I tried to make it interesting because I wanted my students to love social studies as well. We would walk down to the city of Kingston and discuss the Civil War and the part that Kingston played in the war. The students loved talking about the Civil War, and they wanted to remain on this unit the entire school year.

During my second year of teaching, my sister Margaret was hospitalized in Columbus, Georgia. The doctors had given my parents a diagnosis that she would never get well. I remember seeing my stepmom and Dad praying for Margaret. They would place their hands on the television as Oral Roberts prayed and agree with him for Margaret's healing. The doctors were amazed at Margaret's recovery and could not explain it. To God be the glory.

> *"But He was wounded for our transgressions; he was crushed for our iniquities; upon him was the chastisement that brought us peace, and with his stripes we are healed"* (Isaiah 53:5).

At the end of my second year of teaching, one of my students came to me and said that she wanted to introduce me to her brother. I thought that she was kidding, so I just smiled. She was persistent, so again she came up to me and said that her brother and I were going to marry. Now I really thought she was crazy. As it turned out, her brother visited me; we dated, and before long, we were married. He had a daughter, Denise, who I raised. I had always wanted a little girl, so this was perfect.

Because my husband worked in Rome, we decided to purchase a home and moved to Rome. I commuted to Kingston each day. The drive took approximately fifteen minutes, and I thank God that the fifteen years that I commuted from Rome to Kingston to teach, I never experienced car trouble during this entire time. Again, God looked out for me and protected me.

Teaching was simply wonderful, but during the summer, there was nothing to do, so I applied for a part-time job at Sears. I was assigned to the tool department where I not only sold hand tools, power tools, bicycles, treadmills, and worked as cashier, but I learned how to mix paint as well. My intentions were to work one summer, but I remained at Sears working part-time on weekends and during holidays for approximately eighteen years.

During my tenure at Kingston Elementary School, I was voted Teacher of the Year, and I established a Junior Beta Club for students who excelled in their classes. I also taught piano lessons after school, and my piano students preformed beautifully in a piano recital at the end of the school year. They were so proud of their accomplishments, and their parents were equally as proud. I always said something positive about each of my students at the recital. My years of taking piano lessons were finally paying off.

In addition to establishing a Junior Beta Club, I required students to construct social science display boards. Not only did I teach students how to write research papers and construct display boards, I held several informative sessions for parents so that they would have some knowledge of how to help and support their children during this time. I brought in judges from other schools to judge these projects. Students with the most prestigious display boards and research papers were selected to participate in the county social science fair. Kingston School students always did well at the county fair, and one year, a student from Kingston School was selected to participate in the state fair held in Atlanta, Georgia. All the faculty, staff, and parents were so proud because this was a first from Kingston School. Although we did not place in the state fair, we were thankful to have been selected because the stakes were extremely high.

"Oh give thanks to the Lord, for He is good; for His loving kindness is everlasting" (Psalm 107:1).

CHAPTER 8

Additions to the Family

After living in Rome, Georgia, for three years, I became pregnant with my first child. I was very sick and nauseated during the first four months and could keep very little food down on my stomach. Since I was out of school for the summer, I just tried to eat saltines and whatever else I could keep down. This would vary from day to day as my husband was an excellent cook. He had grown up cooking for his family, so he cooked a big meal every day.

Prior to going back to work, I talked to my doctor about my nausea, and I was given medication to take. This medicine miraculously cured my nausea, and I was able to work the remainder of my pregnancy. I had so much fun planning for my little baby girl. My students gave me showers, and gifts were given from relatives and friends.

Because I have O negative blood, my doctor decided to induce my labor and that was fine with me. My husband agreed, and after getting my already-packed bag, we went to the hospital; and after a few hours, our baby was born. I don't remember the birth because I was put to sleep. When I woke up, it was very late; but there was a pamphlet on the nightstand indicating the sex, weight, length, of the baby. My eyes focused on *baby boy*, and that was shocking. I had taken a beautiful pink blanket, pink booties, and a little pink jumper to the hospital to bring my little baby girl home in. My husband just swapped the pink for blue. I have no idea why I thought I was having a girl, but I thanked God for giving us a healthy baby boy, and we named him *Dion*.

> *"Lo, children are an heritage of the Lord; and the*
> *fruit of the womb is his reward" (Psalm 127:3).*

I knew nothing about taking care of a newborn baby, so my husband's ninety-year-old grandmother stayed with us a few days and taught me about caring for a newborn. I was so appreciative because this was a frightening experience for me.

After six weeks, I was required to go back to work. My husband, Freddie, kept Dion until about 1:00 p.m. each day because he worked second shift and had to be at work by 3:00 p.m. He would get Dion up, feed, bathe, and dress him daily. After this, he took numerous pictures of him. Our neighbor Catherine Sparks kept Dion until I arrived home at approximately 4:00 p.m. This was a blessing because we did not want to put him in nursery school until he was at least six months old. Freddie would also keep Catherine's son Seon and take pictures of him and Dion each day.

The following fall, Dion was placed in nursery school. Freddie never took him early in the morning, but he always kept him as long as he could prior to going to work. Dion was never in nursery more than four or five hours a day. This was another blessing.

As Dion transitioned from nursery to kindergarten, we began talking about having another child. Although I was extremely sick during my first pregnancy, I was willing to risk being nauseated because I wanted a little baby girl.

I asked my pastor, Rev. L. C. Ramsey, to baptize me. I had grown up in the Methodist church and I had been sprinkled. So, Rev. Ramsey baptized me, and I found out later that I had been about two months pregnant during this baptism. How great is our God.

Three days after Dion's sixth birthday, February 3, my labor was induced, and our baby girl, Kiara was born. This time, taking pink to the hospital was appropriate. God had already let me know that I was having a baby girl, and so it was.

"Ask, and it will be given to you; seek, and you will find; knock, and it will be opened to you" (Matthew 7:7).

By this time, I thought that I was an expert at taking care of babies, but that was far from being the truth. Kiara did not sleep all during the night like Dion did. My dad told me to give her a little paregoric in her formula, and this solved the problem. Of course, paregoric was only given by prescription, but Daddy could go to the drugstore in Talbotton and ask for a bottle, and he got it. No questions asked.

When I was in college, I always had a desire to join Delta Sigma Theta Sorority Inc. It was during this time that God gave me this opportunity. I wanted to be a part of a sisterhood that was based on Christian principles and dedicated to public service. My cousin Juanita Searcy Skulart, my siblings, Jackie Searcy Nichols and Loretta Searcy Terry, and other members of my family were Deltas. I became a member of the national chapter and the Rome Alumnae Chapter of Delta Sigma Theta Sorority Inc. in 1978.

Denise, Dion, and Kiara grew up participating in church and school activities. All of them did extremely well in school. Denise graduated from high school and enlisted in the Air Force.

As I served as director for the youth at St. Paul, Rev. Poleon Griffin asked if I would organize a "children's church." I gladly accepted, and each Sunday, prior to the youth going upstairs, children's church was held downstairs. They were taught the word of God so that they could understand it. They were also taught respect, what God says about how others should be treated, and other biblical truths.

Rev. Griffin challenged me to train three young men to become worship leaders. Those young men were Regional Mackey, Brandon Jones, and Dion Knox. Rev. Griffin asked that these young men wear a white shirt, tie, jacket, black, blue, or khaki pants when they were in the pulpit leading worship. At this time, Dion was a little chunky, and my husband and I did not have a lot of money. I remember going to Salvation Army; purchasing a black, brown, and blue dress jacket; and getting these jackets dry-cleaned so that Dion could be dressed appropriately. I taught them how to stand and speak with authority, and Rev. Griffin taught them the word of God. Today, two of these young men are ministers. What a blessing!

> *"Train up a child in the way he should go: and when he is old, he will not depart from it"* *(Proverbs 22:6).*

CHAPTER 9

A New School

Bartow County had plans of making elementary schools to house grades 1–6, middle schools to house grades 7–8, and high schools to house grades 9–12. The time had finally come for this vision to be realized. My passion was teaching eighth graders, but I wanted to remain at Kingston Elementary School. I was given sixth grade, and this was fine, but I was not happy teaching sixth grade. So in 1988, after working at Kingston School for eighteen years, I decided to transfer to Adairsville Middle School. Mrs. Barbara Middleton was the principal, and she was a joy to work for. I was the only African American teacher in the middle school, but I was welcomed with open arms. I was given four eighth-grade science classes and one computer class. It is ironic because I did not even know how to turn on a computer, but I learned quickly. My area was not science, but I followed the *Teacher's Edition*, and I did a great job. My second year at Adairsville, the eighth-grade social studies teacher transferred to the high school, and I was given four social studies classes and one language arts class. That was favor.

> *"For you, O Lord, will bless the righteous; with favor; You will surround him as with a shield"*
> *(Psalm 5:12)*

FROM THE PEACH FIELDS TO BECOMING
A UNIVERSITY PROFESSOR

During my tenure at Adairsville Middle School, I was voted Teacher of the Year by my peers. I organized and sponsored the first Adairsville Middle School Junior Beta Club, and a scholarship fund was organized in honor of our former principal, Mrs. Barbara Middleton.

Inspired by God, I encouraged members of the Beta Club to raise money in order to take needy students in grades 6–8 on a shopping spree each December to Walmart. Students were selected by office personnel who had access to confidential information on the family's financial status. Two students from each grade level were selected for this shopping spree. The Beta Club donated a total of $25 to each student, and Walmart in Calhoun, Georgia, matched our donation, giving each student a total of $50. It was a blessing to see these students picking out socks, shirts, blue jeans, and sometimes coats. I noticed that in almost every case, these students selected something for their parents/guardians as well.

> *"But if anyone has the world's goods and sees his brother in need, yet closes his heart against him, how does God's love abide in him?" (1 John 3:17).*

I never viewed teaching as a job, but as a calling by God. I taught social studies, so I organized the first Adairsville Middle School studycade. Students toured Georgia for five nights and six days where they visited historical places such as forts, the lighthouse in Brunswick, the home and church of President Jimmy Carter, the birthplace of President Jimmy Carter, the Okefenokee Swamp, and Andersonville National Cemetery, where more than thirteen thousand Union prisoners died and were laid to rest. Each spring, I took from twenty-five to thirty-five students on this Georgia studycade, and the information that they gained in one week was astronomical. Students were actively engaged and well behaved.

Although prayer was taken out of the schools, I held Bible study in my classroom each Thursday morning prior to the beginning of school. The students arrived at school around seven thirty, and faculty members were always invited to join us. During our moment of silence, my homeroom students observed this time by praying or sitting quietly in the desks. This was my time of meditation and praying as well.

I remember when God saved me. I was singing in the choir, and we were singing a song entitled "Changed." I felt the spirit of the Lord flowing though my body, and from that moment on, I wanted to do what was pleasing to Him, reading his word daily, and learning more about Him.

I have always known the importance of prayer. Each school day, before I left for school and my children left for school, we would gather in the kitchen, hold hands, and pray for God's covering and protection. I thank God that during my travels to school from Rome and Kingston and later from Rome to Adairsville, I never had an accident. I had a flat tire once on my way from Adairsville. God had someone to quickly fix the tire. However, I was stopped by a patrolman for speeding once, but I only received a warning.

"For he will command his angels concerning you to guard you in all your ways" (Psalm 91:11).

I knew that students, and especially middle school students, would become inattentive and get bored if they were not kept on task. So my instructions, I would pause about every twenty minutes and tell my students something comical. This was my strategy for keeping my students on task. Since this was my personality, saying something funny came very easy for me. I can remember my brother telling me that he wondered how I could teach school because I was such a humorous person. In order to teach middle school, you almost need to put yourself in their shoes and get down on their level. I was humorous, yet when it was time to get back to instructions, my students could transition and get back on task.

During this time, I collected elephants. On my bookshelf were elephants of all shapes and sizes. At least once a week, students asked if they could dust and count my elephants. If we had some free time, I gave them permission to do this. This was the highlight of their day. I believe the highest count was over four hundred elephants.

Students and parents brought me elephants for Christmas, for my birthday, and any other time during the school year.

Since my eighth graders were practical jokers, some of them loved to play jokes on me. One such day, I was standing at my podium, teaching. I noticed that the class was unusually quiet and attentive, but I continued teaching. At one time, I glanced over at the bookshelf and quickly noticed an elephant was turned backward. I turned it around and continued to teach. I walked around the class, teaching and asking questions, still not suspecting anything. For some unknown reasons, I walked over to the bookshelf, and to my surprise, all four-hundred-plus elephants were turned around backward. I began to scream, and the students laughed and laughed. Some of them had stayed after school and turned all the elephants around. This was one of the many jokes that they played on me. I loved my students, and I loved teaching.

Kiara began middle school and participated in band in addition to taking ballet, tap, and jazz twice per week. Dion was also a member of the marching band, and he began working at McDonald's mostly on weekends.

During Dion's senior year in high school, he became a member of Leadership Rome, participated in the band, and he was one of the mediators who met with students from West Rome and East Rome as the two schools were being combined.

Dion was selected from among hundreds of students in Georgia to serve as an ambassador for the 1996 Olympics. What an honor this was. He was able to meet other students throughout Georgia as they witnessed the Olympics festivities.

One of Dion's goal was to complete school without missing any days. This goal was achieved as he finished school with perfect attendance from grades 1–12. God was looking out for him.

As graduation approached, Dion sent applications to numerous schools such as Morehouse, Clark-Atlanta University, the University of Georgia, and other colleges. He was accepted at them all, but there was one problem: he was not able to get funds to attend any of these schools. His heart was set on attending Morehouse. He applied for grant after grant with no success.

One day as I was working at my part-time job, Calvin Pritchett came in the store and introduced me to his friend, who worked at a college in South Carolina. Calvin told him about Dion and that he was graduating from high school. This gentleman told me to have Dion fill out an application to Claflin College and send him his transcript. I had never heard of Claflin College before, and South Carolina was a bit far; however, I passed this information on to Dion.

Dion filled out the application and requested that his transcript be sent to Claflin College in Orangeburg, South Carolina. We had no idea what God had in store for Dion. Actually, we forgot about the application as we were still trying to figure out how we were going to manage sending him to the school that he had chosen.

One day, Dion received a letter from Claflin College awarding him a full four-year grant with everything paid except his books. The only restriction was that he maintain a B average. Oh my God! What a *mighty* God we serve!

During the summer, we began gathering things that Dion would need to take with him to college. The day finally came when Dion was to report to Claflin. Freddie, Dion, Kiara, and I got the luggage and other items packed in the trunk and headed out for the long drive to Orangeburg, South Carolina.

After arriving at Claflin, the process of checking in went smoothly. We helped make up Dion's bed and we helped him place his underwear, etc., neatly in the dresser drawers. As any mother would, I separated his clothes in the closet. Shirts and pants by color, blue jeans together, dress jackets by color. I was told that all of that was moved around after we left.

We tried to spread the time that we were there as long as possible, but it was getting late, and we had to get back to Rome. As we began saying our good-byes to Dion, we all became extremely emotional. Freddie cried, Kiara cried, I cried, and Dion cried. One of Dion's roommate's mother came up and comforted us. She assured us that she would make sure that he was taken care of. Reluctantly, we left, but I think we all cried all the way back to Rome. The odd thing about that scenario was when we arrived home, I called to check on

Dion to make sure he was all right, and he was out with his new friends having fun.

> *"For I will pour water on the thirsty land, and streams on the dry ground; I will pour out my Spirit on your offspring, and my blessings on your descendants" (Isaiah 44:3).*

CHAPTER 10

Another Tragedy

The school year went by quickly, and Dion was back home for summer break by the middle of May. The public schools in Rome and Bartow County did not close for summer break until the last of May, so Kiara and I were still in school.

On Monday, toward the end of the school year, I left for school as usual. Around ten o'clock, I received a call on the intercom for me to come to the office because I had a phone call. Freddie had been taken to the hospital, and it was serious. I quickly let the secretary know that I would have to leave and I needed a substitute for my class.

When I arrived at Redmond, Freddie was still in emergency, and they allowed his brother and me to go in his room and sit as he was unresponsive and they were waiting for his doctor to come and examine him. It seems as though we waited forever, but finally, his doctor came and examined him, talked to us, and admitted him. He was taken to ICU a few hours later.

I remained at the hospital day and night, going home only to shower and change clothes. Numerous people came to sit with me and bring me breakfast, lunch, and dinner. I thanked them, but I could not eat anything as I was not sleeping or eating. There were specific times for visiting in ICU, and during these hours, I went into Freddie's room, talked to him, and prayed. Even though he was in a coma, the doctors had informed me that patients who are in a coma-tose state can actually hear what is being said. I prayed and prayed for his healing, but early Saturday morning, May 28, one of the nurses came in the waiting room where I had been waiting for the past five nights and informed me that he was expiring. He had been on life support for the past five days, and his kidneys had shut down. I quickly called my children and family members to ask if they wanted to come in and say good-bye. Dion and Kiara hurried to the hospital, and they were with their father when he breathed his last breath.

"He will wipe away every tear from their eyes, and death shall be no more, neither shall there be mourning, nor crying, nor pain anymore, for the former things have passed away" (Revelation 21:4).

This was not only devastating to me and the children but to family members as well. Freddie's brother had passed a few years ear-lier at the age of thirty-one, followed by his father, then his sister had passed at the age of forty-one. All passed within a few years of each other, and now another sibling had passed, leaving only three surviv-ing siblings. Only one sibling survives at this time.

I began making preparation for Freddie's home going services. This was a task that no one ever looks forward to, but at some time, all will be faced with this. It was decided that the funeral and burial would take place in his hometown of Kingston. He would be buried close to his father, sister, and brother.

The days following the funeral were hectic. There was so much business to take care of. People were still bringing food and stopping by to pay their respects, and that was great because we needed to be around people. Since school had closed in Bartow County, I needed to go and take care of the end-of-the-year paperwork. I dreaded this, but it had to be done in order for me to receive my summer pay.

I waited until teacher post planning had ended before going to the school to complete my paperwork. To my surprise, my friend Sandra Cash had taken care of the majority of this paperwork along with getting my textbooks taken up, counted, and stacked neatly in the book room. What an awesome God we serve. One of my students had left me a large red elephant. I never found out who left this gift, but I still have this elephant today.

"In the same way, let your light shine before others, so that they may see your good works and give glory to your Father who is in heaven" (Matthew 5:16).

When tragedies happen in our lives, it affects individuals differently. I could not find documents that I knew that I had. I had to make decisions that I was not capable at this time of making because I was still grieving. I was concerned about raising my children alone and how I would be able to support and educate them. I knew God, but I did not *know* Him during this time.

The Saturday before Father's Day, I had gone to work at my part-time job and Kiara was at home. We had planned to go and put flowers on her father's grave for Father's Day the next day after church. When I got home from work at about 9:20 a.m., I went to the bedroom to begin getting ready for bed. Kiara was looking at television in the den. Suddenly, Kiara came and stood in my bedroom door and calmly said that there was a snake in the kitchen. I jumped up screaming, stood on the bed, and told her to close the door and get on the bed. I called my neighbor to come and rescue us, but for some reason, he was taking a little too long. I then called 911, who told me that I needed to call the fire department. All I could think about was the snake skittering down the hall to the bedroom and attacking us.

My neighbor finally knocked on the door, and Kiara calmly went to the kitchen (where the snake was), opened the door, and let him in. I screamed for Kiara to come back to the bedroom. My neighbor assessed the situation and asked Kiara where she saw the snake. Kiara told him the snake came from under the stove and went under the cabinet. When my neighbor looked under the cabinet, I heard him say that he saw two snakes. By this time, I was hysterical, and then I heard the fire department pull into the yard. Two men from the fire department came in dressed in outfits that resembled the outfits that I had seen on the movie *Ghost Busters* and retrieved the snakes. When I asked what they did with the snakes, they informed me that they threw them back over in the field across the street because they were only harmless rat snakes. I could not believe what I was hearing. Kiara and I stayed with her godmother that night. I did not want to go back into that house, but I had no choice. I had no other place for my children and me to go. My struggles continued.

> *"A father to the fatherless, a defender of widows, is God in his holy dwelling" (Psalm 68:5).*

CHAPTER 11

Raising My Children Alone

Summer was upon us, and we went about the task of trying to survive without my husband and my children's father. I had to decide what bills to pay and what bills to pay on. I was faced with unexpected bills that I was not aware of until my husband passed. This further depressed me, but my father had taught me to always pay my bills, and I always tried to honor this.

My pastor at that time would talk about tithing each Sunday. I was not interested because I knew that I was going to give my same $20 once or twice a month. One Sunday morning, I decided to listen closely about tithing. My pastor explained what God expected us to give and what God promised. I pondered on this for weeks, and finally, I told God that I was going to tithe one time, and if I was not able to pay my bills, I would not be tithing again. When I received my monthly check from Bartow County Board of Education, I calculated 10 percent, wrote the check, and placed it in the offering plate. From that point on, each time I wrote a check for a bill, it was as if someone was placing more money in my account to take care of the things that my family needed. God's word is true. He does not lie.

"Honor the Lord with your wealth and the first
fruits of all your produce; then your barns will be

filled with plenty, and your vats will be bursting with wine" (Proverbs 3:9–10).

Dion had announced that he would not be going back to school because he felt obligated to take care of his sister and me. I had a long talk with him assuring him that this is what his father would want and that Kiara and I would be fine. This was far from the truth, but I knew that I could not let him know my fears, so I was able to convince him to go back to school and continue his studies at Claflin College. Reluctantly, he gave in; and in the fall, he headed back to Claflin for his second year.

Since there were no buses leaving from Rome to South Carolina, I would drive to College Park, and one of my sisters would take us to the bus station in Atlanta where Dion would catch the bus for Orangeburg, South Carolina. The bus would leave at approximately 12:30 p.m. And Dion would arrive in Orangeburg approximately 6:30 or 7:00 p.m.

Orangeburg was a small town, so the bus station there was always closed, so he would call a cab and wait until the cab arrived to take him to the school. I never wanted him to stand out in the dark waiting for a taxi alone. During daylight savings time, it was better; but when the time changed, it was dark by six o'clock, so I worried until he arrived at the dorm and I received a call informing me that he was in the dorm. He needed a car, but financially, it was impossible.

Likewise, when Dion was able to come home mainly on holidays, Kiara and I would go to College Park where one of my sisters would take us to the bus station in Atlanta. Dion's bus would arrive at approximately 12:30 a.m. After dropping my sister off in College Park, we then drove back to Rome, and it was then well into the early morning, so he came home very few weekends because his stay would only be a Saturday as he would have to catch the bus in Atlanta on Sunday to get back to school.

"Even youths shall faint and be weary, and the young men shall utterly fall, but those who wait

on the Lord shall renew their strength; they shall
mount up with wings like eagles; they shall run
and not be weary; they shall walk and not faint"
(Isaiah 40:30–31).

Dion developed severe eczema over most of his body. He told me that his skin was extremely dry, and he itched most of the, time but he never told me the extent of this eczema. I suggested that he use Vaseline to rub on his skin to help with the dry places.

When Dion came home for Thanksgiving, I took him to a dermatologist, who gave him a prescription for cream that he was to rub on the patches of eczema. The cream was fairly expensive and the tube was small, so Dion had to use it sparingly on the most severe places on his skin. Dion never complained, but I would inquire about his skin when we talked, and he said that each morning when he got out of bed, he would find dry skin in the bed where he had scratched during the night as he was sleeping.

When Dion came home for Christmas, my sister was visiting with us and happened to see Dion's skin. All I had ever seen was his arms and lower legs. She asked to see his body and said that we had to do something to help him. She immediately called a friend, who knew an African American dermatologist in Atlanta who was noted as one of the best in the country. This was on a Friday, and Dion was going back to school that Monday. God can do anything. My sister got the doctor's number, called this doctor's office, and she was able to get an appointment for Dion that Monday before time for his bus to leave. That was nothing but the favor of God.

After seeing the doctor, Dion boarded the bus and headed back to school with medicine that had been prescribed. I can't imagine how he was able to concentrate, attend classes, and keep his GPA up during the time when this eczema was so severe, but he did. After a few days, the eczema began healing, but he had to see the doctor approximately every three months for treatments and a prescription for cream. I had to pay out of pocket for the visits to the doctor, and my insurance reimbursed me very little. The medicine was expensive, so I asked him to use the cream sparingly.

After seeing this doctor for approximately one year, Dion came to me and said that the doctor and medicine were too expensive and he did not want me to continue to pay out of pocket. I looked at him and let him know that I would do what I had to do. He then told me that he had prayed about this and he had asked God to just let him control the eczema. He did not see the doctor again because God answered his prayers.

> *"Now unto Him that is able to do exceeding abundantly above all that we ask or think, according to the power that worketh in us" (Ephesians 3:20).*

The next three years went by quickly. Kiara was in high school, and she was active in numerous organizations. She continued to take ballet, tap, and jazz in addition to participating in the marching and concert band and other organizations. When she reached the age of sixteen, we shopped for a vehicle so that she could drive back and forth to school and practices. This was particularly helpful when the band played at football games in other cities and did not arrive back at the school until 1:00 a.m. or later.

Graduation day for Dion finally came, and in May 1998, Kiara and I drove to South Carolina to witness this blessed event. It was an emotional time for me for many reasons, but I was so proud when his name was called as graduating *cum laude.*

In November of 1998, my grandson Cameron Dion was born, and he is planning to attend college this fall.

> *"And God is able to make all grace abound toward you; that ye, always having all sufficiency in all things, may abound to every good work" (2 Corinthians 9:8).*

CHAPTER 12

A College Professor

Dion came back to Rome and began working full-time, and Kiara was busy completing requirements for completing high school and preparing for college. She had decided on Albany State, and I encouraged her to keep her grades up in order to qualify for the HOPE grant given to Georgia seniors who graduated with at least a 3.0 GPA.

Graduation day finally came for Kiara, and we were all excited and happy that she would be going off to college in the fall. There were many things to do such as purchasing linen for twin beds, purchasing luggage, and all the little extras that students need who are going to be living in the dormitory.

The day came when Kiara was to report to Albany State for orientation. Dion and I drove her, and we had a great time getting her settled in to her dormitory room. As we were about to leave, it hit all of us that Kiara was not going to be at home but away at school. The three of us cried and cried. This was a bittersweet moment.

After thirty years of public school teaching, I had an opportunity to become a college professor. This had been a dream of mine after I began my career in education. We never know how God is going to work in our lives.

I was told that there was an opening at Shorter College for a middle grades professor. I was qualified because I had taught middle grades for years, and I had a passion for middle school students, but

I only had a master's degree. I applied for the position, but I did not hear anything for a while.

After a few weeks, Dr. Clem Slack called and informed me that they decided to hire a gentleman with a doctorate degree. I was fine with that because I only had a master's degree at that time. I signed my contract and was fine with going back to Adairsville Middle School.

One morning as I was heading to school, Dr. Slack called and told me to call the department chair and introduce myself. She said that "we are going to open this thing back up." I had no idea what she was talking about, but I reluctantly called the department chair and told him that I understood that they had already filled the position, but I just wanted to introduce myself to him. He told me that they had not hired the gentleman in question and asked if I would come in for a teaching demonstration. I agreed, and a date and time was set for the demonstration.

On the day of my teaching demonstration, I was a little nervous. There were several professors with doctorate degrees in addition to students majoring in elementary education and middle grades education. I had prepared for this day, and after my teaching demonstration, I felt confident that I had done an excellent job. A few days later, I was called and offered the job as assistant professor of education. Look at how God works!

> *"Every good gift and every perfect gift comes from above, and comes down from the Father of lights, with whom there is no variation or shadow of turning"* (James 1:17).

CHAPTER 13

Retiring from Public Education

Trust in the Lord with all thine heart; and lean not unto thine own understanding. In all thy ways acknowledge him, and he shall direct thy paths.

— Proverbs 3: 5-6

After I received the job offer from Shorter, I retired from Bartow County with thirty years of teaching experience. One year was added to my experience because I had accumulated enough sick leave days to give me an additional year.

I had spent thirteen years and Adairsville Middle School, and I loved teaching social science, reading, and language arts. I had mastered teaming and served as team leader of my team the entire time that I taught at Adairsville Middle. I would miss all the students, teachers, and staff members, but now I would be able to fulfill a dream of mine.

The drive to Adairsville each day for me was very refreshing. It was during these drives that I meditated and talked to God. As I listened to my spiritual tapes, many times I could feel the Spirit of God upon me, and my eyes would fill with tears.

FROM THE PEACH FIELDS TO BECOMING A UNIVERSITY PROFESSOR

"But the Helper, the Holy Spirit, whom the Father will send in my name, he will teach you all things and bring to your remembrance all that I have said to you" (John 14:26).

I began the task of cleaning out closets, sorting through loads and loads of educational material, cleaning out my desk, packing up items that belonged to me, and finally, taking all the elephants off my bookshelf, putting paper around each one, and packing them in boxes so that none of them would get broken. This was a chore, but I finally got everything done with the help of students and coworkers.

My father had taken a turn for the worse, and at that time, he was in the hospital in Columbus, Georgia. Each time that I visited him, I would mention my retirement and my new job. I told him that I wanted him to attend my retirement celebration, but he was called home to be with the Lord prior to the celebration. I had visited him on the day of his passing. My son was with him, and he was talking and smiling. As I turned to leave, I heard Daddy mumble something, and I asked my son what he said. Dion said that he said, "I love you." That was the last time that I saw Daddy alive. We were blessed to have him with us and to see all of us become responsible adults. Rest in peace, Daddy. I love you, but God loves you best.

"Jesus said to her, 'I am the resurrection and the life. Whoever believes in me, though he die, yet shall he live'" (John 11:25).

My retirement celebration was beautiful. A former student of mine and her husband served as toastmasters for this event. Many friends and relatives attended, and several humorous toasts were made. It was hard to believe that I was retiring after thirty years of teaching public education, but I would still be doing what God had called me to do, only on a higher level.

As summer came to an end, I began getting things ready to move into my office at Shorter. Since the décor of my office would be elephants, I purchased curtains, rugs, an elephant end table, and two chairs with rollers were purchased for me from the education department. The weeks prior to the beginning of the semester were spent setting up my office.

All the professors in my department welcomed me and went beyond the call of duty to help me get settled in. They were available to answer any questions that I had about college life and specifically about the education department. I knew that I would love working at Shorter, and I thanked God for giving me this opportunity.

> *"Let the favor of the Lord our God be upon us, and establish the work of our hands upon us; yes, establish the work of our hands" (Psalm 90:17).*

CHAPTER 14

My New Job as a College Professor

I began my job at Shorter in August of 2001, and I found that it was quite different from the "teacher preparation" days that I had been accustomed to for thirty years of public education.

Although I had been given a syllabus for each of my classes when I was in college, I did not understand all that was involved in the preparation. I was first given a lesson on the difference between a *syllabus* and *syllabi* by Dr. Slack. She explained that *syllabus* means one and *syllabi* means more than one.

My assignment was to teach Introduction to Middle Grades Education, literature, reading, and language arts, Social Science for Middle Grades and Secondary School majors, and finally, the field director.

Although I had taught social science, reading, and language arts in middle school, these classes were a little different; so, much studying and planning had to be done in order for me to be prepared adequately for my classes. I searched through numerous textbooks and asked my colleagues for advice. I decided to use the textbooks that the former professor had used for all my classes, thus I worked on my syllabi.

As I used the textbooks to prepare my syllabi, I found that I could use many of the activities that I had used in my middle school classes. Since I would be teaching college students to become middle school teachers, I began to feel more comfortable as I integrated activities with theory. There was still much to be done as I was a neophyte, so I had many questions.

"An intelligent heart acquires knowledge, and the ear of the wise seeks knowledge" (Proverbs 18:15).

Being a college professor was totally different from teaching public school. In public school, teachers are in their classrooms approximately five or six hours each day with an hour or more for planning. College professors are in the classroom only during the time that they have classes; other times, they are in their offices to advise, meet with students, or plan. Professors are also able to leave campus when they do not have classes, unlike public school teachers.

I caught on to schedules, how to prepare syllabi, and teaching on a college campus very quickly. I found that my years of teaching middle school paid off because I could share with my students my experiences as a middle school teacher, and to be honest, I could have written a book on teaching middle school students. I loved my students, and I loved teaching and learning.

In addition to teaching, going to department meetings, faculty meetings, and advising students, I was required to attend conferences. During my first few years as a professor, all my colleagues in the education department attended the GATE conferences. GATE is an acronym for Georgia Association of Teacher Educators. These conferences were held in various cities in Georgia each fall and spring. So much information was gleaned from these conferences, and we were able to talk with other professors and exchange ideas. Dr. Slack and I gave a dynamic presentation during one of these conferences.

"Iron sharpens iron, and one man sharpens another" (Proverbs 27:17).

Prior to the beginning of classes, opening convocation was held where faculty dressed in full academic regalia. It was exciting for me to see the various departments with different colors of hoods and what degree each faculty member had earned.

The first day of class finally arrived, and I was both excited and nervous. I made a copy of my syllabi for each class, so I decided to spend the first day going over the syllabi, discussing expectations, and answering any questions that they student had. To my surprise, some of my students were adults that started college after high school, married, raised their children, and decided to come back to complete their education. I also had students that I had taught at Adairsville.

I have always been a morning person, probably because of my early days of getting up and catching the truck that took me to the peach fields at six o'clock in the morning. My classes the first semester began at nine o'clock and my last class was in the afternoon. When one of my colleagues told me that I could arrange my classes during times that were convenient to me, I changed all my classes for the second semester. My first class began at eight o'clock, and my last class ended around twelve thirty. I also scheduled to teach my classes on Tuesdays and Thursdays. I only taught three classes, as one class reduction was given to me for being the field director.

During my first year at Shorter, I was not required to serve on any committees. This was a blessing because all members of the faculty served on at least three committees that met at least once per month, and sometimes more often, depending on the situation at hand.

> *"But he gives us more grace. That is why scripture says: God opposes the proud but shows favor to the humble" (James 4:6).*

After my first year, I was placed on approximately three committees, one of which was the admissions committee. This was my favorite committee, and I remained a member of this committee until approximately three years before I left Shorter.

It was during my second year at Shorter that I decided to return to school and get my education specialist degree. Dion had graduated from college, and Kiara was now a senior at Albany State. I was still working part-time at Sears, but I felt confident that I could complete this degree in one year. I enrolled at Lincoln Memorial University located in Harrogate, Tennessee. This school had satellite campuses in Tennessee, and classes were held one Saturday each month from eight o'clock to four o'clock. This should have been easy enough; however, I did not realize that although we only met as a group once each month, there was an overwhelming amount of work to be done the other twenty to thirty days of the month.

The year passed by quickly, and we were assigned dates to make our final presentations to the class. Since we only met once each month, we had three classes each semester. As I looked at the date of my group's presentations, I panicked. This was the Saturday of Kiara's graduation from Albany State. There is a policy in the graduate department at Lincoln Memorial that if one day of class is missed, your grade is reduced by one letter grade, and I was taking three classes. This meant that I would receive all Bs, and I wanted to make all As. I decided to take the three Bs and attend my daughter's graduation.

"So shall the knowledge of wisdom be to your soul: if you have found it, there is a prospect, and your hope will not be cut off" (Proverbs 12:14).

Kiara and I graduated the same year. What a blessing. I was further blessed when I was summoned to the provost's office. To my surprise, I was given a check congratulating me on my graduation. Since there was no pay increase for a specialist's degree, this was a token presented to me for my hard work, excellence, and perseverance in going back to school. This was a double blessing.

Shortly after I graduated from Lincoln Memorial University with my specialist degree, Dion got married and moved a short distance away, and Kiara, who was working in Columbus after her graduation, also married, so I experienced the meaning of the empty nest. I had never been totally living alone before, but now, I had to truly trust that God would take care of me. My new job would certainly keep me busy.

FROM THE PEACH FIELDS TO BECOMING
A UNIVERSITY PROFESSOR

Although I was assigned the duty of field director, I had not actually learned all that was involved with this assignment. After several years at Shorter, I was given the task of learning all that was involved in being a field director, and I was given the title of director of Clinical and Field Placements.

After a period, I became a novice in this position that included corresponding with school systems, superintendents, educators, and principals to place students in their schools for observations, practicum, and student teaching. Students were placed according to their major and were required to submit a time sheet to me along with any assignment when observations and practicum were completed. Additionally, prior to placement in the schools for observation, practicum, or student teaching, I was required to make sure that each student had purchased liability insurance and had passed a background check.

Student teaching involved assignments along with observations from college professors. Eventually, students completing practicum were also required to have visits from their college professor. This was always an exciting time for me because it gave me an opportunity to go back into the classroom and observe students who were aspiring teachers and give them suggestions and feedback on my observations.

I was blessed to be among the faculty of Shorter when university status was awarded. All the faculty and staff were excited, and I was now a university professor. I had gone back to school and received a doctorate degree in Christian Education from Jacksonville Theological Seminary. All I can say is, that was *another blessing*. Any time I speak of my job at Shorter, I always give honor to God, because He is the one that gave me the job. It was not of my doing, but it was the favor of God who saw my potential, who looked beyond my faults, and blessed me with what he had called me for from the time I was in my mother's womb.

> *"In him we have obtained an inheritance, having been predestined according to the will of the purpose of him who works all things according to the counsel of his will"* (Ephesians 1:11).

I was asked to pray at open convocations, graduations, and department meetings. God can use you wherever you are, even on your job. I witnessed to numerous students, and I wanted them to see Jesus in me. One such day, a student came to me who was broken. She had been engaged but was scheduled to student teach during the next semester. She had asked her fiancé to be patient as she needed to concentrate on her studies with all of the preparations needed to teach and take the exam for certification. He took this in a negative way and broke off the engagement. When she came to me for advising and to get her student teaching placement, she broke down. I was able to comfort her, pray for her, encourage her, and give her hope. A few days after she left my office, I received a phone call from this student's mother, thanking me for showing empathy to her daughter, but most importantly, for sharing God's word with her. She said that her daughter was going to give up, but changed her mind because I took time to encourage her and let her know that God had a purpose for her and He was going to bring her beauty for ashes.

> *"And let us not grow weary of doing good, for in due season we will reap, if we do not give up"* *(Galatians 6:9).*

As director of Middle Grades, I was required to write numerous reports. These reports included program reviews that determined if the department would be able to continue the program for students to attain certification from the State Department of Education. Students were required to pass certification tests and had a high percentage of students that passed these tests and received teacher certification.

I wrote the modules for two classes during my tenure at Shorter. Those two modules were *Legal Issues in Education* and *Diversity and Multiculturalism*. Not only did I write the modules for these two classes, but I wrote the syllabi and taught these two classes. My favorite of the two was Legal Issues in Education because this class gave students insights on existing laws in education, why former laws were passed, and strategies on how to prevent lawsuits dealing with education.

Each semester, I invited attorneys to speak with student teachers on professionalism in and out of the classroom, the importance of membership in SPAGE or GAE, and who to contact should any issues arise. Students were excited and asked many questions during these meetings. I learned something new that I could emphasize in my classroom each time an attorney addressed our student teachers.

Chapel was held once each week, and guest speakers and ministers shared the gospel with those in attendance. There was a period of praise and worship, and this was a time of prayer and meditation for me. I always began each day with my quiet time with the Lord, so chapel was an exciting time. I thought about the times that I was required to attend vesper services while I was a student at Savannah State. Chapel was not required for me, but I looked forward to attending each Tuesday.

In May of 2015, after fifteen years as a college professor, I left to begin a new chapter in my life. I would be ministering and continuing with God's calling. I was excited about becoming director of Christian Education and further working in the degree that I had earned. I would be ordering Christian material, planning workshops and retreats, and working with youth to encourage them to continue their education after high school, help look for scholarships and financial aid, and set an example as a Christian as well as an educator. God had given me an awesome ministry, and I continued give him the honor, glory, and the praise.

"And my tongue shall speak of thy righteousness and thy praise all the day long" (Psalm 35:28).

CHAPTER 15

God's Gift to Me

February 2010, I received a proposal of marriage. I was so excited because I had not prayed for a husband. I know that God will give us things that we don't ask for, and this was living proof. I thanked Him over and over.

I don't mind waiting, I don't mind waiting, I don't mind waiting for the Lord. I don't mind waiting, I don't mind waiting, I don't mind waiting on you, Lord.

Since we decided to have an August wedding, we had to get busy selecting a venue, making out a guest list, and of course, there was the task of picking out a wedding dress. What fun I had trying on dress after dress until I finally found the perfect dress. Even the price of this dress was more than reasonable, so I knew that this was the dress for me.

I had been widowed for a while and had never really learned to cook very much, so when I was told that it did not matter, this was a blessing. I could cook chicken, fried or baked, green beans, mac and cheese, and a few other simple dishes. My favorite food to cook was cornbread from scratch. I was extremely proud of this dish. I could cook cornbread in the oven, and I could cook cornbread on top of the stove shaped like hot cakes. I tried cooking collard greens, but I could never get them seasoned well.

August 21, 2010, we were married in a beautiful ceremony with friends and family witnessing this union. Since my favorite color was purple, this was the color I chose for my color scheme. Family members gladly served as candle lighters, maids of honor, best men, and my son Dion walked me down the aisle. It was one of the happiest times of my life. With the many struggles in my past, God had given me double, and I would forever remember and praise Him for His precious Gift.

> *"Though one may be overpowered, two can defend themselves. A cord of three strands is not quickly broken" (Ecclesiastes 4–12).*

CHAPTER 16

God's Healing Power

In October 2014, my daughter, Kiara, had outpatient surgery that lasted for approximately six hours. The surgery was a success, and her husband, Delvecchio, and I took her home. She was in a little pain, but she mostly wanted to sleep. Kiara remained at home for a while to recuperate.

When Kiara went back to her doctor for her postop consultation, her doctor told her that he was recommending that she go to Emory University Hospital for observation. When Kiara reported to Emory, numerous tests were performed along with an MRI. She was told that she would need additional surgery.

This is frightening news for any mother to hear, especially when I did not understand why she needed additional surgery so quickly after her previous surgery. I did not let Kiara know how worried I was, but I cried after hanging up the phone. I was told that I had no faith. I knew that God gives us all a measure of faith. I wept because of what my daughter would have to encounter, but I still prayed and believed God for her healing, so I did not understand the connection between the two. I read that sometimes people who struggle with those who cry or have difficulty crying see it as an element of weakness.

Jesus loved Lazarus, and when he saw Lazarus's family and friends that loved Lazarus as well weeping, he was troubled in his spirit. Jesus did not scold them, but he wept also, just as he does with us when he sees us brokenhearted and weeping. He wants us to do the same.

> *"When Jesus saw her weeping, and the Jews who had come along with her also weeping, he was deeply moved in spirit and troubled... Jesus Wept"* *(John 11:33, 35).*

November 2014, I was required to attend a conference in Nashville, Tennessee, to be trained and receive SPA certification to review and approve programs submitted for middle grades education. The conference was held at the Grand Old Opry, and there were numerous vendors there to display various materials on teaching middle grades.

My stepmother had been ill for some time, and at that time, she was in a nursing home in Griffin, Georgia. On Friday night, I received a call informing me that she had passed. She had raised me from the time I was eleven years old, and although she had three daughters and a son of her own, I still tried to do what I could while she was living. Her homegoing services were beautiful.

December 12, 2014, Kiara reported to Emory for surgery. I had prayed along with many other prayer warriors for Kiara's healing. She went through the surgery with no problems. Hot chemo was poured through her stomach for four straight hours, and she was placed in ICU for three days. We were able to sit outside her room in ICU and talk to her and be there for her. The doctors, nurses, and technicians monitored her often, and she was soon moved to a regular room.

Kiara was placed on a liquid diet for a few days, and she was progressing nicely. We walked several times a day even though she was in severe pain. The more we walked, the soreness in her body became less and less. Eventually, Kiara was told that she could eat some solid food, and I remember her ordering chicken strips and fries. She was very hungry because she had not eaten solid food in approximately five days. I bathed Kiara daily, combed and oiled her hair, and I rubbed lotion all over her body. At this time, she had been at Emory approximately six days, and she was excited about when she would be able to go home.

For some reason, Kiara began throwing up everything that she ate. She could not understand why. Her doctors again placed her on a liquid diet, and she was not able to keep this down either. More tests were done, and Kiara was afraid that she would need more surgery because it was feared that there was a blockage somewhere in her body. Again, I was constantly told that I had no faith because of my weeping and concern. I contacted my prayer warriors, and we began praying for Kiara. I had prayed for God to heal her, and I knew that she was healed.

"Heal me, O Lord, and I shall be healed; save me, and I shall be saved, for you are my praise" (Jeremiah 17:14).

The doctors pumped Kiara's stomach to remove any traces of food, and they began the process over again. Again, she was placed on a liquid diet. If Kiara could keep the liquids down, they would slowly began giving her solid food. I prayed for Kiara as well as my prayer warriors. I was still told that I had no faith.

Kiara texted me the following prayer: "Lord, I come to you thanking you for your many blessings in my life. I thank you for keeping me and providing for me in spite of. Lord God, you said in your name, *all* things are possible, so I want to speak healing all over my body. There is no blockage or infection in my body, and everything will start working just fine. Lord God, you said wherever two or three are gathered, you would be in the midst. We give your name the glory, honor, and praise. These blessings I ask in your name for Christ's sake. Amen."

God moved on Kiara's behalf. She began eating solid food, and she began getting stronger and stronger each day. She did not eat much because her taste buds had changed, but she ate something, and it stayed down. After seventeen days at Emory Hospital, Kiara was released to go home and recuperate. This was about three days before Christmas. Praise God! I shared this news with the Sunday school class at the church I was attending, and they joined me in thanking and praising God. Thank you, ladies, for your love and support.

> *"Jesus turned, and seeing her he said, Take heart*
> *daughter; your faith has made you well. And instantly*
> *the woman was made well" (Matthew 9:22).*

When I think about December 2014, I wonder if God was telling me something and I did not recognize his voice or understand what he was saying to me. I have never been a selfish person, nor have I ever wanted everything to be about me. I did what I felt God wanted me to do, but I was criticized. I always had joy in doing for others, many times anonymously. I was so confused, but I continued to believe and pray.

It is so painful when we feel as if we should say things to others to cause them hurt and pain. God wants us to love one another, and even if someone hurts us, we are to be imitators of Christ and pay no one back for what they have done. We should always be willing to apologize to others. God wants us to never mistreat others or cause them to stumble.

> *"The Lord shall fight for you, and ye shall hold your*
> *peace" (Exodus 14:14).*

CHAPTER 17

June 10, 2015

Let all bitterness and wrath and anger and clamor and slander be put away from you, along with all malice. Be kind to one another, tenderhearted, forgiving one another, as God in Christ forgave you.
—Ephesians 4:31–32

When I was in college, I was required to take numerous history classes because my major was sociology. My professor quizzed the class on these dates, so in order to pass the class, I memorized the dates and forgot the majority of them after taking the final exam. When I began teaching social studies, I vowed that I would only require my students to memorize a few important dates.

June 10, 2015, is a date that I will remember for the rest of my life. On this date, my life was shattered and torn, and this brought about depression, brokenness, low self-esteem, and a sense of worthlessness.

I have never been a perfect person, but I took pride in my work, how I dressed, my love for other people, and my giving spirit. I had raised and educated my children primarily as a single parent, I had worked two jobs for over eighteen years, and I had gone back to school to obtain an education specialist degree and then a doctorate degree while working a full-time job. But on this date, none of this mattered because the words that were said to me were cruel and damaging, and I believed them. I could not get the hurting words out of my mind or out of my spirit.

> *"Let no corrupt communication proceed out of your mouth, but that which is good to the use of edifying that it may minister grace unto the hearers"* *(Ephesians 4:29).*

I was told that I was weak, that I had no faith, that I was clingy, that I was fake, that I had been in church all my life and I still had not grown, that it was all about me, that I was no longer wanted, that I was nobody, and so many other hurtful things that are too painful to write. To further humiliate me, I was told shameful and hurtful things about me and intimacy. As tears ran down my face, I asked for prayer and forgiveness, but the answer was no. I knew that God's word tells us that we are to forgive others just as He forgives us, so this was confusing for me. For a period, this same person expressed to me that they were depressed, and cruel things were said; and I always said positive things to build and encourage, and now, hurtful, painful, and damaging words were being said to me from the person that I had encouraged.

As I tried to gather some of my belongings, blinded by tears, I was told that I just wanted someone to feel sorry for me. I cried harder as words of profanity were yelled at me over and over. I silently whispered "Jesus" over and over and over as I needed Him to help me make it home with only a few dollars in my purse.

> *"Likewise the Spirit helps us in our weakness. For we do not know what to pray for as we ought, but the Spirit himself interceded for us with groanings too deep for words"* *(Romans 8:26).*

I had had many struggles in my life, but this was different. This was an affliction that put me in total depression. I could not eat, I could not sleep, I could not pray, I could not attend church, I could not face people because I was embarrassed and ashamed. I stayed in bed, and my son came by each day to literally feed me what little food that I would eat.

I felt that I was a bad person and no one could make me feel differently. I had to be a bad person because no one would say the words that were said to me to anyone unless that person was the worst person in the world. So, I knew that everybody felt that I was a horrible person.

I had prayed and prayed prior to June 10, 2015. I always believed God could do anything. But now, I had nothing and no one but my children. I did not see the hand of God in this at all. I asked God why I had no one to call me, to come and see about me in my time of need when I had always tried to be there and support them when they were going through storms? I had tried to support many by sending a love offering from time to time. I supported others by encouraging them, talking with them, and praying for them. Believe it or not, when going through struggles and storms, it helps to just have someone to talk to. I was no longer needed now so I felt so alone.

> *"Bear one another's burdens, and so fulfill the law of Christ" (Galatians 5:15).*

> *"And we urge you, brothers, admonish the idle, encourage the faint hearted, help the weak, be patient with them all" (1 Thessalonians 5:15).*

After several months, still broken, I got up one Sunday morning, showered, got dressed, got in my car, and stopped at the first church that I came to. I walked in reluctantly, but I found everyone to be friendly, and I was welcomed with open arms. Since I had not eaten properly for months, I became weak and faint. I went to the ladies' room and remained in there so long that the people who were sitting on the pew with me began to worry about me. I made my way to the door, opened it, and asked the ushers to help me. There was a nurse that sat me down and gave me juice. They wanted to drive me home, but I told them that I just I made it home safely.

> *"O Lord, how long shall I cry for help, and you will not hear?" (Habakkuk 1:2).*

I had always attended church while growing up. I served as Sunday school secretary, and I played for our junior choir. After I finished college, married, and moved to Rome, Georgia, I attended and joined St. Paul Baptist Church where Rev. L. C. Ramsey was then the pastor. I loved attending church and working in the church. I put up bulletin boards, served on numerous committees, taught Sunday school, Bible study, served as church treasurer, CEO, sang in the choir, served as director for the youth, and any other duty that was assigned to me by the pastor at that time. I knew that God had blessed me with many spiritual gifts that I had used to edifying the church, but now, I felt that I was not even saved.

I had quit my job as a professor at Shorter University, so I had nothing to do. Education was my life, so I applied for job after job, but the answer was always no. I had no dental insurance, and this added to my depression. I began volunteering a few days a week at the hospital. This gave me an opportunity to be of service to others. My first day of volunteering, I went in the nutrient room to fill up cups with ice and gather bottles of water and canned drinks on my cart to deliver to the patients when I became faint and weak. I slumped over the cart and remained there for a while until I could get to the door and get help. All the nurses ran to see what was wrong, but I could barely talk. Someone quickly put me in a wheelchair and rushed me down to emergency.

> *"Reproach has broken my heart and I am so sick.*
> *I looked for sympathy, but there was none, and for*
> *comforters, but I found none" (Psalm 69:20).*

After I was placed in a room, I called my son and Ruth Jones. Both came and sat with me as I was being examined. After blood was taken and sent to the lab, the doctor came back in the room and said that I was severely dehydrated. I had been eating and drinking very little, and it was now taking a toll on my body. I was given fluids intravenously and told to make sure that I drank plenty of water after being released.

God is faithful. He is faithful to his word and will never, ever, break any of his promises. God knows and sees the big picture when we can only see what is before us at the moment. God loves all His children, and He is our help in the time of storms and afflictions.

"If your law had not been my delight, I would have perished in my affliction" (Psalm 119:92).

With God, I was able to continue volunteering. After checking with numerous companies, I was able to get some reasonable dental insurance. I thank God that I did not cancel my State Merit Health Insurance because once that is cancelled, you cannot get it back. God was still taking care of me.

I begged a pastor to lead me to Christ because I felt that I was not saved. This was basically what I was told June 10, 2015. I believed this, and I wanted to be saved and receive God's forgiveness for the horrible things that I was accused of. I was reminded again as with so many times by my therapists that hurting people hurt other people. God wants us to use our tongues for building up and not tearing down.

Although I was still hurt and broken, I continued attending Sunday school, church, and Bible study. I cried a great deal, but God began using people to help me with my brokenness. I was asked to teach Sunday school. I did not feel worthy to teach in God's house because of the horrible person I was told that I was. After much praying, I agreed to teach. With the numerous ladies that attended this church and had been members for years, I wondered why I was asked to teach.

In order to teach God's word, one must study God's word. I always had my quiet time with God daily, praying and reading his word, but now I had to really study to show myself approved. I now know that God was preparing me for another assignment.

"If any of you lacks wisdom, he should ask God, who gives generously to all without finding fault, and it will be given to him" (James 1:5).

My next assignment was to teach a women's class on Sunday evenings for six weeks from five o'clock to six o'clock. This was challenging for me because I definitely did not feel worthy of this assignment. I accepted the challenge, and numerous women signed up to take this class. I was nervous, but after studying the material and reading, I understood why God used me to teach this group. The title of this study was *Brave: Honest Questions that Women Ask* by Angela Thomas-Pharr. This study looked at the heart of women and their feelings. It was such a powerful study, and as I taught these lessons, I witnessed the brokenness of these women, and I realized why God had chosen me to lead this group. I felt each lady's pain because I too was broken. God does answer prayers. His answer is yes, no, or "Wait. I have something better for you."

"The Lord is close to the broken-hearted; he rescues those who are crushed in spirit" (Psalm 34:18).

My doctor had been concerned with my kidneys for some time. She ordered a series of tests and found that there was protein in my urine and blood. This was a result of problems with my kidneys, so an ultrasound was ordered. The ultrasound revealed that there was a mass on my right kidney.

An MRI, CAT scan, and bone scan and numerous other tests were ordered, and I prayed for God's healing. After meeting with the urologist about my kidneys, it was decided that the entire kidney would need to be removed. This surgery would be serious, but I looked on the positive side because it could have been worse. All the depression for the past two years with the dehydration further damaged my kidneys, and protein had leaked into my blood in addition to the kidney problems. I thought about how God had brought me through the last two years with the hurt, brokenness, depression, and rejection, so I put it all in His hands.

Again, the devil tried to convince me that I was being punished; but this time, I knew that I could fight him with the word of God. Prayer is the key. Families should pray corporately and individually. If this does not happen, Satan steps in and has a field day as he destroys that relationship. Don't let this happen to your family. Pray together daily.

"For where two or three are gathered in my name, there am I among them" (Matthew 18:20).

CHAPTER 18

My Testimony

So I take pleasure in weaknesses, insults, catastrophes, persecutions, and in pressures, because of Christ.
—*Philippians 1:12*

I cannot count the number of times that I was told that I am who God says that I am and not who man says that I am. Because of the terrible things that were said to me, I believed who man said that I was. For so many months, the pain was unbearable. It was a pain that I had never experienced before, and it left me weak and helpless. It took me a long time to finally say positive affirmations, and it took me many months after this to believe these affirmations. Only then was I able to allow God to help me to accept that everything I had been told was not of Him, but of Satan. Satan comes to steal, kill, and destroy. Satan is real and walks around daily, devouring and destroying people, churches, and families.

It was not my affirmations that ultimately helped me, but it was God's power that worked through me to help me believe that He is who He says He is and He does not lie. When the Holy Spirit is working in us, we become aware of our wrongdoings; and because we want to honor God, we make an effort to change. The old cliché that time heals all wounds is untrue. Time does not heal wounds, only God can heal wounds.

As followers of Jesus Christ, we are equipped with the power of the Holy Spirit. It does not mean that we will never have adversities, but it means that we will not have to face these adversities alone.

God speaks to us whether we listen or not. If God is speaking to you to apologize, don't put it off. I feel that forgiveness and sincerely apologizing are essential to healing. I was listening to a sermon where the pastor said that he was about to give communion. He talked to the congregation about not taking communion, if there is something that they had against another person, and a gentleman walked out of the church. The following Sunday, he asked the gentleman why he left, and the gentleman told him that he left to drive to another city to apologize to a friend that he had wronged years before. The word of God will convict so heed to God's word.

When you make a promise to God, it is important to keep that promise. Never allow anyone to cause you to do anything that you have promised God that you would not do. The word of God tells us in Numbers 30:2 that *"if a man vows a vow to the Lord, or swears an oath to bind himself by a pledge, he shall not break his word. He shall do according to all that proceeds out of his mouth."*

I learned that when adversities come into our lives, this is God's way of getting our attention because He loves us. Satan tries to convince us, especially through our thoughts, that God has abandoned us, but Romans 8:28 tells us that *"in all things God works for the good of those who love him."*

God can see the big picture when we can only see what is in front of us. He is not punishing us when we go through trials and adversities. He is protecting us from something that we cannot see. I had to believe that God had everything in his hands and was looking out for me. I had to begin praying for those who hurt me. For months, these prayers were not real; but as I began spending more time with God, a transformation took place and my prayers became honest and sincere. The scripture tells us in Luke 6:28 that we should bless those who curse us and pray for this who mistreat us. This is not a suggestion; this is a mandate from God and this is what I began doing daily. A very good friend of mine once told me that when you honestly pray for others, God turns around and blesses you. At that time, I could not understand this, but now I know that this is true.

From the months and months that I cried, I eventually had to rely on God's promise in Psalm 126:5 that those who sow in tears shall reap in joy. God counted every tear that I shed and recorded them in His book. From the brokenness, hurt, rejection, and shame that I experienced for over two years, God healed me and gave me the peace that he promised.

> *"There are six things which the* LORD *hates, yes, seven which are abominations to Him. Haughty eyes, a lying tongue, and hands that shed innocent blood, a heart that devises wicked plans, feet that run rapidly to evil, a false witness who utters lies, and one who spreads strife among his brothers"* (Proverbs 6:16–19).

Keep hoping, keep believing, keep praying, and keep doing the right thing. If God could bring me out of the hurt, brokenness, words that were said to me that I thought that I would never be healed from, shamefulness, and feelings of worthless, He can do the same thing for you. God is faithful, and if you keep trusting Him and doing what is right, He will bring you through any situation. It took me two years to really believe that I have faith. God gives each of us a measure of faith, and all we need is faith that is the size of a mustard seed. That is tiny!

> *"Because you have so little faith, I tell you the truth, if you have faith as small as a mustard seed, you can say to this mountain, 'Move from here to there' and it will move. Nothing will be impossible for you"* (Matthew 17:20).

Do I still think about that awful day in June? Yes, and many times I still weep, but I can now thank God for shielding and protecting me from what could have happened. Because of His grace, he snatched me from the danger that I was not aware of. God knows all, and He sees all. He protects us even when we have no idea what we need protecting from.

"When someone does something bad to you, do not pay him back with something bad. Try to do what all men know is right and good" (Romans 12:17, NLV).

So my word for all who have been hurt by others, abused, rejected, shamed, and discouraged: Never retaliate against them, but instead we must do as Jesus commanded His followers to do. Jesus expects us to live like him and respond like He responded when He was being persecuted. We all know his words, and I encourage you to speak to the Father and ask Him to forgive them, for they know not what they do.

I thank God for strengthening me through my struggles, and my tears have been turned into a testimony to help and encourage other women who are hurting. Bishop T. D. Jakes said that "the real praise comes when we start thanking God for what could have happened but didn't, because of his swift grace. Nothing in life happens to us, it happens for us."

"We have heard of your fame; we stand in awe of your deeds. Repeat them in our day; in our time make them known" (Habakkuk 3:2).

ABOUT THE AUTHOR

BARBARA S. COTHRAN is the eldest of five siblings and is a native of Talbotton, Georgia where she grew up and attended elementary school and graduated from Ruth Carter High School in Talbotton.

Dr. Cothran attended Savannah State College and received a Bachelor's degree in Sociology. She began teaching in the Bartow County School where she received Teacher of the Year at Kingston Elementary School and Teacher of the Year at Adairsville Middle School.

She was married to the late Fred L. Knox. They have two children, Chederick Dion Knox who now resides in Cartersville, Ga. and Kiara Loud who resides in Phoenix City, Alabama. She remarried in 2010.

Dr. Cothran received a Master of Education Degree from Berry College in 1978, An Education Specialist Degree from Lincoln Memorial University in 2003, and a Doctor of Ministry Degree in Christian Education from Jacksonville Theological Seminary in 2005.

Much of her Christian foundation was with the St. Paul Missionary Baptist Church of Lindale, Georgia where she attended faithfully for over forty years. Currently she attends Fellowship Baptist Church of Rome, Georgia.

Dr. Cothran retired from public education in 2001 and began working at Shorter University where she was Director of Middle Grades Education and Director of Field and Clinical Placements. She wrote modules for two classes while at Shorter and worked with administrators to teach Introduction to Middle Grades Education classes at Rome Middle School in order for students to get a feel of middle school students prior to student teaching.

Education and ministry continue to be strong focal points in her life.

CPSIA information can be obtained
at www.ICGtesting.com
Printed in the USA
FFOW04n1347250218
45233669-45819FF